I Need Your Love
—Is That True?

I NEED YOUR LOVE
—Is THAT TRUE?

How to Stop Seeking Love,

Approval, and Appreciation

and Start Finding Them Instead

Byron Katie

Written with
Michael Katz

Harmony Books
New York

Library of Congress Cataloging-in-Publication Data
Katie, Byron.
   I need your love—is that true? : how to stop seeking love, approval, and
appreciation and start finding them instead / by Byron Katie, written with
Michael Katz.—1st ed.
   1. Self-actualization (Psychology) 2. Interpersonal relations.
I. Katz, Michael, 1945– II. Title.
   BF637.S4K334   2005
   158.2—dc22   2004028485

ISBN 1-4000-5107-X

Printed in the United States of America

Design by Meryl Levavi

10   9   8   7   6   5   4   3   2   1

First Edition

To Adam Lewis,
with love and gratitude

CONTENTS

Love is wonderful—except when we are searching for it, trying to hold on to it, or missing it. Hours of every day are taken up with difficult, painful thoughts about our relationships. This book introduces a way of relating that is much easier than our usual approach, and more effective. Through its guidance and exercises, you will learn how to have a fulfilling love life, and you will find out how you can be in charge of your own happiness.

of love? This chapter includes an exercise that allows you to discover what your experience of love really is—an experience that doesn't disappear and doesn't depend on anything or anyone outside you.

This chapter points out what happens when you form a romantic relationship based on a fictitious identity and a false concept of love. It exposes the widely held myth that love is about getting what you want and having your needs met. It also includes exercises that allow you to clearly see the difference between wanting and loving.

Chapter 6 gives you many examples of how relationship troubles disappear when you're willing to judge your partner mercilessly and then question your judgments.

Apparent flaws in your partner are opportunities for self-realization. What you see as a fact may be just another unquestioned thought. The chapter ends with a conversation in Amsterdam that transforms a divorce into a love story.

If you believe that you absolutely need someone, that you couldn't make it without that person, that the people around you or life in general is failing to give you what you want, this chapter offers powerful ways to come to your own aid.

The real-life story of a couple who saved their marriage through inquiry.

10. WHAT'S NOT TO LOVE? COULD IT BE YOU? 203

There's nothing left now between you and love except what
you haven't resolved inside yourself. This chapter facilitates the
process of discovering what that is. It shows you how to free
yourself from what you're most ashamed of, what you can't forgive, what you still resent, what you want to hide, and any criticism you can't welcome with open arms.

11. LIVING IN LOVE 220

What does love look like when it's not about seeking, wanting,
and needing? Excerpts from the accounts of hundreds of people
who are living the discoveries that make up this book.

12. LOVE ITSELF 245

A description of the experience of love when it is so firmly estab-
lished in you that there is nothing outside it.

FURTHER TOOLS FOR INQUIRY 247

ACKNOWLEDGMENTS 255

FOREWORD

by John Tarrant

Author of *Bring Me the Rhinoceros
and Other Zen Koans to Bring You Joy*

The interesting thing about Byron Kathleen Mitchell (yes, she really was named Byron at birth—Byron Kathleen Reid) is what she has discovered and has to teach about love. It's something extraordinary, and this book will show you how it's done. Once you see it, it's obvious and will change your life if you try it out. It works for me. Also, just so you don't think that she is different from other people in some special way that makes her capable of doing things you couldn't do, it might be good to learn something about her. That way you might be able to see that what she has to teach can work for others, especially you. Her life has been ordinary and difficult and successful and full of misjudgment and intelligence, just like most lives.

When wise people return out of the desert in the old stories, they have lots of hair, are usually dressed in robes—which is what everyone wore in the desert—and they can't help speaking about what they have found out. In the United States, such wise people might look much more ordinary to us, have, say, big hair, long fingernails, and a background in real estate. Byron Kathleen Mitchell (everyone calls her Katie) has a background in real estate, and though she no longer has big hair and now wears Eileen Fisher clothes, she still can't help talking about what she discovered.

She does actually come from the desert, from Barstow; that's the first thing in the creation myth of this discovery. Barstow is in the Mojave Desert in Southern California, the last stop before the long haul into Arizona. It has railway sidings and a nearby Air Force base and neat rows of houses where military personnel cultivate flowers in front yards in sight of the desert. The Mojave is bleak even by desert standards; it lacks the whimsy of cactuses, yet becomes truly beautiful if you start to pay attention to it. If you take a walk with Katie there at sunset, the warm wind seems like a caress and the rocks are subtle in their shades of brown and yellow and black and red, and the shadows are blue. She will lead you up canyons to places where hidden water drips and you might begin to see the desert as kind and believe her when she says it was her teacher.

Her story is hers, yet it is an everyperson story. She was happy with three children and a husband who loved her and a business, and then she became unhappy—gradually at first, and then all at once. She gained a lot of weight, she began to drink, she became angry and afraid, she slept with a revolver under her pillow. The revolver under the pillow is not as unusual in Barstow as it would be in San Francisco, yet it was disquieting to her family. She kept her business going but was helpless in most other ways and felt deeply unworthy. So far, this is an ordinary sort of story and an ordinary kind of pain, though severe: you wander along through life taking in the view until something hits you on the side of the head and gets your attention.

The interesting part of the story usually starts at the moment you fall off your donkey, and so it does for Katie. Her crisis was profound and didn't seem to be resolving itself. It was a crisis of her whole being. Her family wondered if she was going mad. She checked herself into an eating disorder center because it was the only kind of treatment her health program would pay for—a nice, practical, American touch. This absurd idea turned out well. She just stopped everything for a while. But it wasn't a therapy or a treatment that helped. She just woke up one morning and the world turned over, and with it her heart did too. She had been knocked off her donkey on the road to Damascus, and her life would never be the same. This was in 1986.

It was one of those sudden, intense, and transforming experiences that happens for no good reason, and in Asia is called enlightenment. Suddenly everything was turned around. Where before she was afraid and desperate, now she felt love and kindness in every moment. Everyone was astonished, especially her kids. They say that the difference was like night and day. They could tell immediately that they didn't have to be afraid anymore. Suddenly she was loving, she listened to them, she wasn't angry, she was delighted with their lives, and this helped them to become delighted too.

But just what had changed? Katie made a really simple discovery. She noticed that she had been believing her thoughts and terrifying herself half to death with them. Then she stopped believing her thoughts, and the world stopped at the same time. The inner conflict and fear dropped away. Straightaway, she felt deeply for others in the same plight and wanted to explain what she had seen. This feeling of connection and love was the beginning of a method to help others.

Here it is in her words:

> *I saw clearly, irrevocably, that everything was backward, upside down from what I believed. My thinking had opposed everything as it truly was and reacted with stories of how I thought it should be. "My husband should be more honest." "My children should respect me more." Now I saw that instead of seeing what was happening, I was placing conditions on what was happening—as if I had the ability to dictate reality.*
>
> *It was clear to me now that the truth was the extreme opposite. My husband should not be more honest—because he wasn't. My children shouldn't respect me more—because they didn't. Instantly I became a lover of reality: I noticed that this felt more natural, more peaceful.*

And for the rest, how do you live when you are happy? Well, some things changed a lot: She lost weight, and her anger and sadness were gone. Other things don't look so unusual from the outside. She married again. She keeps in close contact with her kids, who do the usual ordinary and surprising things children do—her daughter has a couple of children and Katie tells the stories of being at their births. One of her sons likes to ride motocross bikes and produces interesting rock music in Los Angeles, another is an electrician with three kids. Family life.

Something that changed completely is Katie's work life. After her world stopped, she greeted the people she met with such freshness and presence that people in Barstow started to talk about a lady who was "lit"—as if she had a glow inside. They would start talking to her about what gave them pain, and she would bring them home, make them a meal or a cup of tea, and sit them down on the sofa. She would have them write down their troubling thoughts, then she would introduce them to her questions, beginning with, "Honey, is that true?" Katie didn't tell anyone what to do or what to believe. They answered her questions for themselves. In turn, people's lives changed—some quickly, some slowly.

From this intimate beginning, her teaching spread as she was invited to other places in California and then the world. She has taught pretty much everywhere—from Osaka to Cape Town, taking in Jerusalem and San Quentin prison on the way. Thousands and thousands of people. People pass on what they have learned to their friends, and in this way her work spreads. Her method has remained pretty much the same, though now she doesn't get as much time to cook. She still calls people "Honey" and sometimes "Sweetheart," terms she uses comfortably, as a mild blessing. What she does is to sit down with someone, and have them write out the thoughts that give them pain. Then she asks her questions. Katie always starts with the thoughts a person has about others, thoughts around love or approval or appreciation or admiration—the tangled feelings that people have for each other at work or at home. What happens in the human heart is the field of her wisdom and the place she brings kindness and clarity to. If enlightenment is an interesting thing to you, she has made it available without going to a monastery or into the desert. Her questions help integrate the natural wisdom we all have when we are not being chased around by fear and anger.

Here's the way Katie herself describes her discovery:

My life was like this fable: I walked into the Mohave Desert on a gorgeous day, minding my own business. Suddenly, Oh my God!—there's a big fat Mojave Green rattlesnake directly in front of me. And I had almost stepped on him! No one around for miles and this could be a painful, slow death. My heart was beating to pop out of my chest, my brow had broken into a sweat, I was paralyzed by fear.

But then, and I don't know how it happened, my eyes began to focus: I dared another glance at the snake—and miraculously, I saw: It's a rope! That snake is a rope! *Well, I fell to the ground and began to laugh, cry, and to just take it in. I even had to poke it.*

What had happened? I knew one thing: I was safe. I knew that I could stand over that rope for a thousand years and never be frightened of it again. I felt such gratitude and ease. The entire world could come upon this snake, scream, run away, have heart attacks, scare themselves to death—and I could just remain here fearlessly, and pass on the good news. I would understand people's fears, see their pain, hear their stories about why it really is a snake, and yet there would be no way that I could believe them or be frightened of that rope. I had fallen into the simple truth: That snake is a rope.

The way Katie tells it, it doesn't matter how miserable you are; what matters is if you begin to question the thoughts behind your unhappiness. There is something you are taking to be a rattlesnake that is really a rope. Confusions about relationships are all forms of the same fear—that you won't survive or be happy without someone else's approval or love, that if you are not working twenty-four hours a day to please your boss, your spouse, your colleague, things will fall apart. Katie shows that there is another, less desperate, much easier way to get love.

How do I help people who think that the rope is a snake? I can't. They have to realize it for themselves. They could take my word for it, because they want it to be true. But until they see it for themselves, they would always in their hearts believe that the rope is a poisonous snake and that they are in mortal danger.

Well, thoughts are like that, and inquiry is about the snakes in the mind—the thoughts that keep us from love and from the awareness of being loved. I can see that every loveless, stressful thought in the mind is a rope. Inquiry is meant to help you discover for yourself that all the snakes in your mind are really and truly just ropes.

Katie's best discovery is that when you do question your thoughts, you find out that the world is a much kinder place than you had imagined, and there's no need to go to sleep in fear or wake up anxious. When you really start to look, the world is full of love, and there's plenty to go around.

Santa Rosa, California
December 2004

PREFACE: HOW THIS BOOK WAS WRITTEN

"Can you imagine?" That's what I thought the first time I met Byron Katie. I wasn't sure what I was meeting—was it Mary Poppins crossed with a Zen master? A brisk, incisive, loving, alert, and cheerful woman. I was there to discuss becoming her literary agent, but I had trouble sticking to the agenda because we laughed so much. At one point our host actually laughed so hard that he fell off the couch.

Even with my limited exposure to Katie's method of questioning your thoughts, it seemed to me that it changed everything. We laughed at what would happen to government, education, marriage, if people questioned what they believe. I was more interested in this conversation than in getting a book out. A book—*Loving What Is*—finally did appear. And five years later, I'm still being struck by its implications, and I still have trouble sticking to the agenda when I talk with Katie.

Katie spends most of her time on the road leading various kinds of workshops, and in that role she doesn't have to explain much. She asks people to trust her questions, and she demonstrates how they work. She meets every thought that comes up—agonized or angry or sad—with the same inquisitive and friendly "Is that true?" Her warmth and acceptance do the rest. They allow her to move quickly without much explanation. She soars.

When Katie asked me to help her write this book, I saw it as my job to be more of a plodder, to walk along on the ground, making sure to clarify the intervening steps on the page. Here and there I would add a layer of explanation or an exercise. In other places I couldn't resist pointing out things that Katie doesn't usually talk about directly. For instance, as part of my job as an agent, I keep up with the drift of popular self-help books. I began to notice that, based on what I had learned applying inquiry to my own life, the best course often seemed to be the exact opposite of what the self-help books advised. Katie got a big laugh out of that, even though I don't think she's ever read a self-help book.

In the explanatory sections and in the connections that I occasionally spelled out, I introduced passages to the book that Katie wouldn't have written. Yet when she read them, they excited her, and she interjected her own comments and thoughts. We sent passages back and forth by e-mail, and met often. As a result, parts of the book came out in a hybrid style, like a rocket-boosted bicycle.

My hope is that you'll do as I have done—take a test spin on that bicycle. Ask yourself Katie's questions. There is really no way to describe what will happen when you do.

Michael Katz

I Need Your Love

—Is That True?

INTRODUCTION

⚬

Everyone agrees that love is wonderful, except when it's terrible. People spend their whole lives tantalized by love—seeking it, trying to hold on to it, or trying to get over it. Not far behind love, as major preoccupations, come approval and appreciation. From childhood on, most people spend much of their energy in a relentless pursuit of these things, trying out different methods to be noticed, to please, to impress, and to win other people's love, thinking that's just the way life is. This effort can become so constant and unquestioned that we barely notice it anymore.

This book takes a close look at what works and what doesn't in the quest for love and approval. It will help you find a way to be happier in love and more effective in all your relationships without being manipulative or deceptive in any way. What you

learn here will bring fulfillment to all kinds of relationships, including romantic love, dating, marriage, raising children, work,
and friendship.

In the course of reading this book, you'll begin to notice how
many of your thoughts are about the quest for love and approval—
something most people never discover. And just by noticing,
you'll learn a whole new way of relating to your thoughts. This
will radically change how you are with yourself and with anyone
important to you: your spouse, your children, your parents, your
boss, colleagues, employees, friends. You won't have to learn a
new way of presenting yourself that isn't true for you or that
deceives others. Instead, you'll be pleasantly surprised by what
you discover. You'll be amused as well.

If you're in pain right now because your quest for love and
approval has hit a bad patch, you'll find it helpful to follow the
exercises in this book. They work best when, just for a moment,
you put aside your desire for relief from pain and do them in the
spirit of a search for truth. Relief will come quickly if you can
find what is really true, not for other people but for you. This
isn't a book of advice. Instead, it offers you questions that will
bring you face-to-face with parts of your life that you may not
have thought about until now. Getting to know yourself in this
way is interesting, and bursts of natural light and happiness will
appear where you least expect them. All you have to do is genuinely answer the questions you'll find here. And if you do
answer them from your heart, you'll discover for yourself what
you've always wanted and how effortlessly you can get it. Many
of you will get it simply by reading this book.

Here is one way of understanding where the journey of this
book leads. Consider a smile. First think of a deliberate smile,
the smile you produce when you think you should—for instance,

for a photo. That smile is useful in some ways; it's intended to be kind to others, like Secretary Appreciation Week.

Now think of a smile that happens by itself. This smile can't be produced on purpose, it can't be faked, and there is no instruction book for creating it. We all love a smile that happens by itself. Unmistakably genuine, it opens doors and hearts everywhere.

Even if it is seldom allowed to see the light of day, you know that this smile is somewhere inside you, ready to burst out. It comes from an enjoyable conversation that you have with yourself. Once you understand this, everything in your life with other people will change. The book you're about to read is designed to introduce you to that conversation and, if you like, to help you make it your own.

1

DO YOU BELIEVE
WHAT YOU THINK?

✤

Have you ever felt that the harder you look for love, the more it seems to elude you? Or that seeking approval makes you feel insecure? If you have, there's a reason. It's because seeking love and approval is a sure way to lose the awareness of both. You can lose the awareness of love, but never love itself. Love is what we are. So, if love is what we are, why do we look for it so hard, and often with such poor results? Only because of what we think—the thoughts we believe that are not true.

You don't have to believe any of this. You can verify it for yourself as you read this book or when you put the book down and ask four questions about your own relationships, or lack of them, and discover how your life changes.

In the pursuit of love, approval, and appreciation, what do

we think? We think that the love and approval of others are the keys to the kingdom—to every good thing in the world. We think that seeking romance brings love, a sexual partner, long-term closeness, marriage, family. And we think that trying to impress society—trying to win the admiration of the right people—is our best shot at bringing fame, wealth, and satisfaction into our lives.

So we think that if we succeed in the quest, we're home: safe, warm, and appreciated. And what if we fail? We're homeless, out in the cold, lost in the crowd, unnoticed, lonely, and forgotten. If those are the stakes, no wonder the quest can be so fearful and all-consuming. No wonder a compliment can make your day and a harsh word can ruin it.

The big, primitive fears rarely rise to the surface. Few people walk around actually thinking that they're about to fall through the cracks of society and vanish. Instead, thousands of anxious thoughts appear all day long: "Was I noticed?" "Why didn't she smile?" "Did I make a good impression?" "Why hasn't he returned my call?" "Do I look okay?" "Should I have said that?" "What do they think of me now?" It's a constant monitoring to see if we're gaining or losing ground in the grand approval sweepstakes. Those little doubts are rarely noticed or questioned, and yet they set in motion hundreds of strategies designed to win favor and admiration, or just to please. The unspoken belief is that unless people approve of you, you're worthless.

The irony is that the struggle to win love and approval makes it very difficult to experience them. Chronic approval seekers don't realize that they are loved and supported not because of but despite their efforts. And the more strenuously they seek, the less likely they are to notice.

How do we get into this predicament? For a few pages, we'll just look at the ways unquestioned thoughts create our experience. We'll see how often-unnoticed thoughts that most of us share lead us to needing, wanting, longing, and reaching for what we already have. The thoughts behind a familiar 3 a.m. anxiety attack are a good place to start.

Thought at 3 a.m.: Nothing Supports Me

Suddenly you wake up in the middle of the night, glance at the clock, and wish you were still asleep. A thought appears: "What's going to happen to me? It's a cold, uncaring universe. I don't know what to do." These thoughts were triggered by a mutual-fund commercial you saw last night, but you don't realize that. And the next ones come from a half-remembered motivational tape: "There are no guarantees in this world. Nothing's going to happen for you unless you make it happen." This thought provides a little boost, followed by a major deflation as you remember that self-reliance hasn't worked all that well for you. "I need so much. I have so few resources to get it. My survival skills aren't great, and basically I'm faking it. I'm helpless and alone. " The next thought brings some hope: "If I could just get more love from my family and friends, if just one person really adored me, if my boss really believed in me, then I wouldn't be so anxious, and I could count on being supported."

The thought "Nothing supports me without my efforts" is just one of the unquestioned and often unnoticed beliefs that set in motion the search for love and approval. Let's pause for a moment and explore the opposite.

Daylight Reality Check:
Everything Supports Me

Do you know what supports your existence right now?

Just to scratch the surface of this, suppose you've eaten your breakfast, sat down in your favorite chair, and picked up this book. Your neck and shoulders support your head. The bones and muscles of your chest support your breathing. Your chair supports your body. The floor supports your chair. The earth supports the building you live in. Various stars and planets hold the earth in its orbit. Outside your window a man walks down the street with his dog. Can you be sure that he isn't playing a part in your support? He may work every day in a cubicle, filing papers for the power company that makes your lights come on.

Among the people you see on the street, and the countless hands and eyes working behind the scenes, can you be sure that there is anyone who isn't supporting your existence? The same question applies to the generations of ancestors who preceded you and to the various plants and animals that had something to do with your breakfast. How many unlikely coincidences allow you to be here!

To explore this for a while, look around and see if there is anything you can say for sure *doesn't* play some role in supporting you. Now look again at the 3 a.m. thought "Nothing supports me without my efforts." In this moment wouldn't it be more true to say, "Everything supports me without my efforts"? The proof is that here you are, sitting in your chair, doing nothing, being fully supported.

Everything supports you whether or not you even notice it, whether or not you think about it or understand it, whether you love it or hate it, whether you're happy or sad, asleep or awake, motivated or unmotivated. It just supports you without asking for anything in return.

Right now, sitting in your chair, as you breathe, notice that you're not *doing* the breathing, you're *being breathed*. You don't even have to be aware of it, you don't even have to remember to breathe, because that is supported too. Complicated and intricate as your requirements for existence might be, they are all being met. At this moment there's nothing you need, nothing you need to do. Notice how it feels to take in that thought.

Now think of something you *don't* have. I'm sure you can think of something. . . .

The Thought That Kicks You Out of Heaven

The thought that kicks you out of heaven could be "I'd be a little more comfortable if I had a pillow." Or it could be "I'd be happier if my partner were here."

Without that thought, you're in heaven—just sitting in your chair, being supported and being breathed. When you believe the thought that something is missing, what do you experience? The immediate effect may be subtle—only a slight restlessness as your attention moves away from what you already have. But with that shift of attention, you give up the peace you have as you sit in your chair. Seeking comfort, you give yourself discomfort.

What if you did get a pillow? That could work (if you have a pillow). You may find yourself back in heaven again. It may be the very thing you needed. Or you could pick up the phone and convince your partner (if you have a partner) to join you, and maybe he or she would actually arrive. And perhaps you would

Heaven: "This is wonderful. I could stay here forever."

Hell: "This is not quite perfect."

be happier, and perhaps you wouldn't. In the meantime, there goes your peace.

The thought that kicks you out of heaven doesn't have to be about comfort or happiness. It could be "I'd be more secure if . . ." or "If only it could always be like this," or it could be just the thought of a cup of coffee. Most people are so busy making improvements they don't notice they've stepped out of heaven. Wherever they are, something or someone could always be better.

So, how do you get back to heaven? To begin with, just notice the thoughts that take you away from it. You don't have to believe everything your thoughts tell you. Just become familiar with the particular thoughts *you* use to deprive yourself of happiness. It may seem strange at first to get to know yourself in this way, but becoming familiar with your stressful thoughts will show you the way home to everything you need.

Getting to Know You

When you begin to notice your thoughts, one of the first things you'll see is that you're never alone. You're not alone with your lover or with anyone else; you're not even alone with yourself. Wherever you go, whomever you're with, the voice in your head goes with you, whispering, nagging, enticing, judging, chattering, shaming, guilt-tripping, or yelling at you. When you wake up in the morning, your thoughts wake up with you. They push you out of bed and follow you to work. They make comments about people at the office and people in the store. They follow you to the bathroom, get into your car when you do, and come back home again with you. Whether or not someone is waiting for you at home, your thoughts will be there waiting for you.

If you're afraid to be alone, it means you're afraid of your thoughts. If you loved your thoughts, you would love to be alone anywhere with them; you wouldn't have to turn on the radio when you get in the car, or the TV when you get home. The way you relate to your thoughts—that's what you bring to every relationship you have, including the one with yourself.

But Wait a Minute!

You may be asking: "That voice in my head, isn't it me? Don't *I* think my thoughts?" You can answer this for yourself. If the voice in your head is you, *who's the one listening to it?*

When you wake up in the morning, you may notice that by the time you realize you're thinking, you're already being thought. Thoughts just appear. You're not *doing* them. Occasionally you may have the experience of waking up before your thoughts. The mind spins for a few seconds seeking to know what it is, and then the world restarts in your thoughts, piece by piece. "I am so and so. This is Philadelphia. That person next to me is my husband. It's Tuesday. I need to get up and go to work." That process happens continuously when you're awake. Thoughts create your world and your identity in every moment.

What Do Your Thoughts Have to Say About Love?

If you listen to your thoughts, you'll notice that they are telling you what love can do for you. For instance, after a disappointment in love, you may have a raw and exposed feeling. Your thoughts may tell you that you've been deprived, that you are abandoned, excluded, empty, lonely, or incomplete. They may

Your most intimate relationship
is the one you have
with your thoughts.

tell you that only love can make you feel good again. If you're fearful, if you crave safety and security, your thoughts may tell you that love will rescue you. If life is disappointing or doesn't make sense, many people think that love is the answer to that as well. It would be useful at this point to see what you think. Just ask yourself what you hope for or expect from love, and make a list of five things you think love will bring you.

Most people believe that *love* and *need* are synonymous. "I love you, I need you" is the hook of a thousand love songs.

If you ask yourself what you really need in life, you'll probably come up with a list like the one you just made about love. People ask for the same things as they go through life. The *way* they ask just gets a little more sophisticated:

> Mommmyyyy!
> Mine!
> Gimme!
> I want . . .
> I need . . .
> Please . . .
> I need your love.
> You're not fulfilling my needs in this relationship.
> I need you to . . .
> I can't go on without . . .
> These are my requirements . . .

Thoughts about your wants and needs can be very bossy. If you believe them, you feel you have to do what they say—you have to get people's love and approval. There is another way to respond to a thought, and that is to question it. How can you question your wants and needs? How can you meet your thoughts without believing them?

I meet my thoughts the way I would meet my husband or my children: with understanding.

2

QUESTIONING YOUR THOUGHTS ABOUT LOVE

∽

Thoughts and Feelings
in the Pursuit of Love

It may seem odd at first to look at grand passions or unhappiness, especially unhappiness about love, in terms of thoughts. Still, if you slow down and take a look, you'll find that there is always a particular thought that triggers any stressful feeling. Anxiety about love is the result of simple, childlike thoughts, thoughts that everyone has, even ninety-year-olds. "I need your love." "I'd be lost without you." Unquestioned thoughts like these pretend to guide you toward love when in fact they are obstacles to it.

People who are upset sometimes say they can't locate the thought that is causing the upset; they can only feel a flood of emotion. This doesn't mean that the thought isn't there. Suppose, for example, you say something heartfelt and he doesn't reply; he just gets up and leaves the room. You're left sitting there feeling as though the world has ended. The thought may be "He isn't interested in me." It may become "Why do I bother? No one really cares about me."

If you aren't feeling upset right now, as you read this, remember a past situation in your life where you were very upset; be still and allow that feeling to re-create itself. If you're upset and you can't seem to find the thought behind the emotions, try this: Take some time to travel inwardly toward the place where the feeling is most intense. This means sinking into the physical sensation of the feeling. Let yourself be upset all over again, for your own sake, and this time give it a voice. If the feeling could talk, what would it say and who would it say that to?

Don't rush this. Be precise. Otherwise you're likely to come up with something that seems wise or kind—the thought you think you *should* be thinking—instead of the thought that's really there and hurting.

Suppose you've just returned from traveling for a week with a new friend, and your hopes for the experience were completely dashed. A psychologically correct thought, such as "My expectations were too high," isn't what you're looking for when your real feelings are saying, "You let me down," "You hurt me," "You lied," "You're not the person you pretended to be." Your actual thought, the one you blurt out in the moment like a child— write *that* thought down as bluntly as you can. That's the thought you're looking for.

Often, within pain or depression, there are thoughts you've had for so long and held so close that you don't even know they are there. And you've never stopped to see if you even believe them.

What if you stopped to ask? What if you had a method of

seeing whether you really believe your most disturbing thoughts? The Work—it's also called inquiry—is exactly that. Seeing it as a method is only temporary. After you do inquiry for a while, you find that it becomes automatic—your natural way of relating to thoughts. Believing your thoughts comes to seem more and more *un*natural, a method of fooling yourself, and it becomes clearer and clearer that inquiry returns you to reality.

How do you bring a thought to inquiry?

Introducing The Work on Seeking Love and Approval

Before the actual instructions for bringing a thought to inquiry, we'll take a tour of the process, so that you can get a feel for it.

IS IT TRUE?

After you've found the thought that's upsetting you, the first step is to ask if it's true. That means checking it against your own truth, going inside yourself and seeing if you really believe the thought that's troubling you. Does the thought match what you know as reality? In most cases it doesn't.

There's no reason to believe that thoughts match reality. As you move through life, thoughts appear like shots in the dark. They are no more than vague attempts to figure out what's going on around and inside you. When you're seeking love and approval, many thoughts are aimed at deciphering the behavior of the people you care about, or theorizing about what's going on in their minds.

In a sense, every thought poses a question, something like "Is *this* what's going on?" A thought about something we perceived, if it were expressed accurately, might say, "I think he insulted me—is that what happened?" But, like children, we tend to focus on the alarming part: "He insulted me." We grab hold of it, then react as if the thought were a fact. We go into pain, or we attack, instead of answering the question implied by the thought "He insulted me—is that what really happened?" (What if the reason he didn't answer your friendly wave is that he didn't see you because he wasn't wearing his glasses?)

HOW DO YOU LIVE WITH AND WITHOUT THAT THOUGHT?

Any feeling of discomfort or stress is an alarm that lets you know you're believing an untrue thought. In this step, you first examine what happens when you believe your thought. You notice in detail what the thought does to your emotional and physical life. Suppose, for instance, that your thought is "George doesn't care about me." Take a good look at how you live when you're in the grip of that thought. How does that thought affect you? How do you treat yourself and others, including George, when you believe that thought? Do you pity yourself? Do you feel hurt and angry? Is this where you become a victim? Do you stop talking to George and give him "the look"? Do you snap at your colleagues or your kids? Does it affect your sleep?

Then you take an imaginative leap. You imagine what your life would be without the thought: if you didn't believe it or if you were incapable even of thinking it. Just for this moment, don't bother about whether or not the thought is true. The point is to experiment, to see what your life feels like when you don't believe that thought. In your imagination, look at George without the thought "He doesn't care about me" and stay with that experience for a while.

This step lets you notice the consequences of believing a thought. You thoroughly immerse yourself in life *with* the thought, and then you give yourself a taste of life *without* it.

TURNAROUNDS: IS THE OPPOSITE AS TRUE?

This is the final step of inquiring into the thought. Like a mirror, the mind has a way of getting things right but backward. So you take your thought and turn it around. This means literally reversing it in as many ways as you can. You then ask yourself if these reversed versions seem as true as or truer than your original thought. They often do.

Let's turn around the thought "He insulted me": first to *the other*, then to *the self*, then to *the opposite*.

> *I* insulted *him*. (I jumped to my conclusion when he didn't wave, and I judged him harshly.)
>
> *I* insulted *me*. (I turned a possibly innocent action into an insult. *I* was the one who created the insult, in my own mind. And my angry thoughts made me feel small and mean.)
>
> He *didn't* insult me. (Maybe he didn't even see me. Maybe he was thinking of something else. I can't really know what his intention was.)

When the mind wants to prove that it's right, it can get further into a rut, like a stuck car. Trying out turnarounds and considering whether they may possibly be true is like rocking your car back and forth to free it from the mud.

Suppose, for instance, you're convinced that it would be a terrible thing if your boyfriend were to take a job a thousand miles from where you live. This thought leaves you paralyzed with anxiety. Turning it around makes you look at a possibility that your stuck mind would never consider: Are there any ways it could be a *good* thing if your boyfriend took the job and moved away? Your mind may refuse to even look at that possibility. That is pure stuckness.

But what if you can find even one genuine reason to support the reversed thought? Perhaps you can find this: your boyfriend's new job could be tremendously fulfilling for him, and your relationship may improve because of that. If you can see even a slim possibility that this may be true, the fear has to lessen. Maybe his absence would allow you to spend more time with your friends, or to start working out, or to take the course you've been wanting to take. Maybe his move to an exciting city would result in your spending time with him there, or even moving there—who knows? You don't have to believe these reasons or act on them— just *finding* a reason can move you out of your rut. You may be astonished at the lightness and relief that come from opening your mind to the possibility that what you were convinced was terrible may not be so terrible after all.

You may resist this exercise because you believe that it would somehow bring about what you fear. In the example above, you may think that opening your mind to your boyfriend's move, even for a moment, would make you a weaker opponent of it. But if you really look at that thought, the opposite is more likely: When people take a fearful and rigid stance, they often bring about what they're trying to prevent. Turnarounds open more space. They allow you to see how things can work out in a peaceful way, beyond what you had considered when you were defending a position.

If someone has trouble finding one reason to support a turn-around ("This is a terrible setback and that's that," "This could work out for the best? No! I won't even consider that!"), I often suggest that they find *three* reasons that the turnaround could be true. When your mind refuses to budge, you may discover that finding three genuine reasons, even if they seem silly or insignificant at first, moves you out of your rut and puts you back on the road to interesting possibilities.

How to Do Your Own Inquiry

Now that you've read the overview, here are the instructions.

1. When you feel disturbed, upset, or simply unhappy about some situation in the present or the past, notice the thoughts that are running through your mind, and write down the one that is upsetting you the most right now. If you're convinced that it's a feeling, not a thought, give the feeling a voice. Write down what the feeling would say, as a short, simple statement. For example, "He just walked out the door, and that means he doesn't care about me." Just writing down the thought that's been tormenting you is a powerful act. Now you can question it.

2. Ask *you* if it's true. "He doesn't care about me"—is it true? Don't ask if the thought matches what you've been told or have learned. Don't consider the way life is supposed to look. (He didn't put down the newspaper when you came into the kitchen; he didn't call to tell you he'd be late; he walked out the door without saying goodbye—but can you be sure that any of this means he doesn't care about you?) Don't consult the part of you that knows what the answer *should* be. The question is, does the thought match what you know inside? Does that thought resonate with your deepest sense of reality? Can you *absolutely* know that it's true that he doesn't care about you? ("I don't know" is as good an answer here as "yes" or "no.")

3. Explore how you live when you believe this thought. Overall, does this thought bring peace or stress to your life? Does it bring you closer to the people you love, or does it separate you from them? How do you react when you believe the thought "He doesn't care about me"? What does it feel like to believe it? How do you treat yourself and others? How do you treat him? Take your time with this process. Picture yourself believing the thought. Do you react with sadness? Depression? Anger? Do you withdraw from him? Do you try to win him over? Do you judge yourself and feel like a failure? Do you light up a cigarette or head for the refrigerator? Be as precise and detailed as you can be.

4. Explore what life would be like without the thought. Use your imagination to give yourself a glimpse of who or what you would be without this thought. Don't look for a better thought to substitute for the painful one. Just live for a while in the space that opens up when you view your situation without the old thought. Pretend that you don't have the ability to think the thought. What would that be like? Look at him in your mind's eye without the thought "He doesn't care about me." Maybe you will simply see a man who is deeply absorbed in reading his newspaper, who loves his wife but doesn't want to shift his attention to her right now. Maybe without the thought "He doesn't care about me" you'll find it easy to take pleasure in his pleasure.

5. Turn the thought around. Consider reversed or opposite versions of the thought. If a certain turnaround doesn't make sense to you, don't bother with it. Turn the original statement around any way you want to until you find the turnarounds that penetrate the deepest.

Turning around "He doesn't care about me":

I don't care about *him*. (When I feel hurt, I withdraw or I get angry, and I don't care what he feels.)

I don't care about *me*. (I don't care about myself when I go to war against someone I love. I take away my own peace of mind. I put myself in a hostile situation, I create an enemy for myself, I give myself a lot of stress and sadness. This is when addictive behavior such as bingeing, smoking, or overeating begins to kick in.)

He *does* care about me. (He may love me and still speak harshly to me. He may love me and still want to leave me.)

Ask yourself if any of your turned-around versions seem as true as or even truer than your original thought, and if they do, find three genuine ways in which each of them is true. Turnarounds can dramatically set you free from a thought, especially if you've loosened your belief in it by following the earlier steps.

Ask Four Questions and Turn It Around: The Pocket-Sized Reminder of The Work

Whenever you have a stressful thought, these four questions and the turnaround will guide you through your inquiry:

Is it true?
Can I absolutely know that it's true?
How do I react when I think this thought?
Who or what would I be without the thought?
Turn the thought around, and find three genuine
  examples of how each turnaround is as true as or truer
  than the original statement.

This pocket-sized version will get you started. If you come across any thoughts that persist in disturbing you, you'll find a complete troubleshooting manual on page 247.

I don't do thoughts; they do me—
until I question them.

3

SEEKING APPROVAL

A child is happily absorbed with her own games in the playground. All of a sudden she shocks herself by performing a flip. Kids around her, whom she had barely noticed, are laughing and clapping. She repeats the flip to see if they'll clap again. All over the playground, kids are going, "Look at me! Look at me!," happy when they get the response they want, disappointed when they don't. The first child isn't sure what she's discovered, but it feels exciting. She thinks perhaps she's found the key to being included. She goes to work on a new flip with a motive that she didn't have before. She's no longer fooling around to amuse herself. Her focus has shifted to the response she wants from the others, and with that comes the anxiety that she won't get it.

By the time we leave childhood, a lot of us are still doing

flips of one kind or another, seeking approval from almost everyone we know—our partners and children, our parents, our colleagues at work, even the stranger in the elevator. Seeking approval becomes so much a part of our lives that it's automatic: We hardly know we're doing it. It's easier to notice the anxiety it creates out there among our friends and colleagues: This one is chatty and amusing when she's with you but quiet when her fiancé is around. That one at work is always sucking up to the boss. This one has to be the center of attention. This member of the yoga group is particularly calm and smiley when the teacher is around. That one is a doormat for her kids.

Your attention may be drawn to this behavior because what's supposed to be going on isn't. A dinner party that was meant to be an opportunity for friends to relax and get to know one another turns into a stiff ordeal of competitive posturing. A business meeting intended to solve a problem becomes instead an opportunity to impress a visiting executive. Why? Because approval seeking has moved to center stage.

If your curiosity is aroused, you'll find yourself guessing at the unspoken thoughts behind this state of affairs. It's not hard to imagine the thoughts that make your friends anxious, because the same thoughts live, or have lived, somewhere in everyone's mind: "He'll reject me if he sees what I'm really like," "I can't be happy unless someone notices me," and so on. You may or may not act on these thoughts, but if you look inside, you'll probably find them.

In the last chapter, we saw that we don't have to believe the thoughts that pass through our minds, even if they look like facts. In the following chapters, we'll search out the often hidden beliefs that underlie casual interactions, friendships, and relationships at work, and you'll have opportunities to see if they are true for you. Then we'll do the same for falling in love, forming couples, committing to marriage, and love relationships. We'll watch what happens to relationships built on the shaky foundations of our own unquestioned beliefs, examine why they so often fall apart, and see that there is another way.

You can read this part of the book like a novel, just watching other people's quest for love and approval with horror or amusement. But stop to notice when the thoughts behind the stories feel like your own. These are entry points for your own awareness. Your relief from suffering—your freedom—begins when you discover *where you believe these thoughts in your own life*. To find the thoughts, you may have to work backward from some painful happening. "Why can't I forgive him after all these years?" "Why don't I get off the phone with him even though I want to?" "Why couldn't I just tell her the truth?" If you can track down the thought that caused one of these painful or awkward events, you can begin your journey home. These are the thoughts that, unquestioned, lead to separation and misery. When you find one of them, you can ask if the belief is really true. You can notice how you suffer from it. And you can find the peace and the love that are already present inside you when you don't believe the thought.

The Masquerade for Approval

MAKING AN IMPRESSION

We'll begin our exploration with a thought that most people believe: "You need to win people over to make them like you." Whole industries are built around this thought, and it seems obviously true. But is it? Let's take a look.

Winning people over is supposed to begin with the first impression you make. Trying to impress someone, as the word implies, means that you are pushing toward an image you want to print on her mind. Perhaps you just want her to think you're an honest, forthright person, or that you're smart, or that you're attractive. You want to impress that on her. It's as though you're coming up to her with a big rubber stamp and trying to print that favorable image of yourself on her mind. If you can impress that image on her, your relationship is off to a good start. That's a thought that a lot of people believe. But is it true?

One way to check its reality is to notice how you feel when someone tries to impress you. What do *you* see when someone comes at you with a big rubber stamp? From your perspective, the stamp says, "I really need you to like me" or "I want something from you." You may only be a little put off, and you may try to start a conversation. But what if he keeps coming at you with his I-need-you-to-like-me stamp? After a while you give up, or if you really want to figure out who this person is, you have to find a way around his efforts to impress you.

Do people's attempts to impress you actually help you to like them? Is it even useful to think that you need to form an impression of anyone? How in fact do you make up your mind about people? You watch and listen while they say what they say and do what they do, and then, when it's ready to, your mind makes itself up.

BECOMING AWARE OF YOUR OWN SEEKING

Exercise: Beginning to Notice Your Thoughts

By the time we're adults, approval seeking becomes a kind of second nature, and it can be hard to see how much of our mental life it occupies. Here are a few ways you can begin to notice.

Telephone calls are a good place to start. The person on the other end can't see you—but you can see yourself. Watch your thoughts as you pick up the phone to call someone important. Do you have a plan for the call? Is there a particular way you want to appear to the other person? Notice the thoughts that flash by in that moment.

As you think about situations like this, what feelings do you associate with them? Locate where you actually feel these feelings. Track them; notice how much of your body they take over.

Before a face-to-face encounter with someone important to you, do you imagine the scene to come? Do you rehearse clever comments, sketch out what you'll mention, suggest, talk about, avoid talking about?

During encounters, do you have anxious thoughts about your standing in the other person's eyes? "Why is he smiling? It could mean he doesn't believe me." "Why isn't she smiling? It could mean she's bored. What can I do to fix that?"

Afterward, do you conduct mental postmortems to review how it went? Do you try to figure out when you scored or lost points and what you should have said or done? Do you enjoy this, or is it stressful?

In romantic situations do you have thoughts like these? "Did she notice me?" "Does she think I'm a phony?" "Did I say the right thing?" "Should I have kissed her?" "Should I pretend to like his apartment?" "Has he stopped loving me?" "Is she leaving me?" "He doesn't love me for who I am." "She doesn't really want to be with me."

In this exercise, there's no need to do anything with these thoughts. Just notice what they are.

We're all children when we believe unquestioned, nursery-school thoughts. "He doesn't like me." "He's a bad person." "It's not fair." "I need to be punished." "I'll cry to get what I want." "I'm a victim." "You are my problem." Have you graduated yet?

Exercise: Noticing What Happens
When You Believe Your Thoughts

Deliberately listen to your own thoughts as you talk with others. What happens when you believe these thoughts? Notice when you try to manipulate with explanation, qualification, or justification, or when you tell anecdotes in the hope that people will think about you a certain way. Notice how you try to manipulate with your face, voice, eyes, your body language, your laugh. Go to a place in your life—it could even be today—where you were seeking love and approval from someone. What did you do or say that was painful to you when you were seeking love and approval?

Now, in writing, answer the following questions:

1. What did you want from that person? List your agenda.
2. How did you attempt to manipulate the way that person saw you? Make a list of the ways.
3. How did you want that person to see you specifically? Make a list.
4. Did you lie or exaggerate? Give examples. What did you say? Be specific. Make a list.
5. Were you really listening to that person or were you more interested in having him or her see how interesting, attractive, or bright you are?
6. What didn't you like about seeking love and approval? Make a list.
7. What did you like when you resisted seeking love and approval?

It can be embarrassing, even overwhelming, to look at your own approval seeking. When people do this exercise in my nine-day school, they have one another's support, so it can be easier. I ask for a volunteer to read out his or her results in front of every-one else. Everyone discovers that there's nothing unique about the most shameless examples they wrote down. We have all experi-enced these things, because there are no new stressful thoughts; everyone has them.

Here is an example from my school. It may help you realize that whatever you discover, you're not alone. The woman who stood up found that her constant approval seeking didn't stop even while doing the exercise:

I ended up writing this exercise about doing the exercise. I didn't pick a specific situation because I saw that I do it all the time. I wanted to do it perfectly to win the approval of all of you.

What did I want? I want you to like me, love me, think I am great, to find me interesting, to find me special, to find me better than others, to find me cute, to say I am lovely, to say I am wise. And [*pointing to a man in the audience*] I want *you* to think I am sexy. And where is that beautiful young woman? [*Scanning the room*] Where are you? Ah . . . I want *you* to think I am young, and I want all the other beautiful young women in this room to think I'm mature enough to know more than you. I want all of you here, representing all the people in the world, to think I am beautiful. I want you all to include me and make me belong. I want you all to appreciate me and to hear me. I want you to need me. I want you to seek me out in the future. I want you to never forget me. I want you to see me as a wonderful, sensitive, caring, witty, articulate, very strong person who is good at everything.

Did I try to manipulate the way you see me? Yes, I did. In the way I speak, in the way I move, in the way I stand, in the way I smile, or in the way I don't smile, in the way I widen my eyes or lick my lips, in the way I look at you, and in the way I don't look at you, in the way I stand close or move away. Did I lie or exaggerate? Plenty. In most situations I try to come across as a little bit better than you. I am doing exactly that right now.

Did I listen? No. I didn't really listen. For instance [*speaking to a participant*], I didn't really listen to you last night; I was just waiting for you to finish so I could put on the show of me again.

Did I get your approval? I don't really know if I got yours, but I know I didn't get mine. I let myself down, and I knew it. It left me empty and insecure, unfulfilled, and always wanting more. I doubt everything about myself. I am sure that I wasn't good enough. For instance, in this particular moment, I wonder what Kirstin actually said. I missed it.

Can I think of a time when I resisted seeking love and approval? Nothing comes to mind at this moment. But I can imagine that it would be really intimate, that there would be authenticity, love, honesty, and no thought of gaining anything.

Here is the next volunteer's story about looking for approval after her father's funeral. Does it seem extreme or quite familiar?

What did I want? It was the day after my father's funeral, and I wanted Carl to kiss me and tell me that he loved me, to forget about his wife and just be with me. I wanted him to see me as vulnerable, in pain, fragile, womanly, greatly in need of him, just yearning for him. I used my pain to try to seduce him. I tried to convey to him, "Don't reject me right now. Look how sad and fragile I am." I exaggerated my grief. We were coming back from the cemetery, and he gave me three poems. I actually felt quite at peace then in the car as I displayed for him the pain, the tears, and the sadness I had suffered in the last week.

Did I listen to him? I wasn't really listening to him. I didn't really care about the beautiful poems he gave me or how compassionate his eyes were, or even how much he was actually supporting me. I just wanted him to do what I wanted him to do: "Hug me right now. Kiss me right now. Tell me you will leave everything for me."

Did I win his love? In the end I did get hugs and kisses, but they were forced. I felt that I stole them from him. It was sad. I felt like a man! I hated myself for using the pain of my father's death to manipulate love. I felt low, pathetic, and desperate. And I was ashamed of my desperation.

Can I think of a time when I resisted seeking love from that person? Six months ago I sent him an e-mail to warn him that I would be at an event where he would be with his wife. It was just love, with no motive beyond it, just my concern about something I knew could surprise or hurt him.

How did I feel? Clean, and so much closer to him than when my every word was a confidence trick.

Exercise: Getting Dressed to Kill

Imagine a situation where you want to wear your best clothes or buy a new outfit (all the way up to wanting a complete makeover). Picture yourself getting dressed for the big meeting or date, and as you put on each of your key items of clothing (you know which ones they are—your new blouse, your favorite tie, your silk underwear), ask yourself about the job you want it to do. "With this blouse, I want you to think that _____ ." Fill in the blank with what you want someone to think, say, or do. Even your socks have an interesting story to tell.

Take a look at the parts of your preparation that are designed to cover up or conceal anything—signs of aging, extra weight, and so on: "I am hiding or disguising this so that you won't think that _____" (or "so that you will think that _____").

Now determine exactly what you don't want someone to think and do. Ask yourself what's the best that can happen if your outfit does its job, and the worst that can happen if it fails.

Some of what you notice may seem ridiculous, and you may resist going on with the exercise. That's a good sign; there's a lot of silliness in the search for approval. Do you really believe any of the thoughts you noticed? How much stress and effort do you feel when you're dressing to kill? Imagine getting dressed without any of those stressful thoughts.

PRETENDING TO BE INTERESTED

If you haven't questioned the belief that it's possible to win people over, and your manipulative charm doesn't seem to be working, you'll think there's something wrong either with you or with your technique (or with both). You may buy one of hundreds of self-help books that teach you how to market yourself—for instance, the multimillion-copy best-selling classic *How to Make Friends and Influence People,* by Dale Carnegie. The author's main suggestion is to make yourself interested in people because, he says, that's guaranteed to win them over. If you find it difficult to do that, he has an alternative recommendation: *Pretend* to be interested. How is that done? Smile, remember the names of their children and dogs, write down their birthdays in your organizer so you can send everyone cards, and also pretend to agree with what they say. It's all about impression management.

Carnegie didn't stop to ask whether fake interest can win real friendship, because his objective was different: He was teaching a sales technique. And it caught on. You meet the results everywhere. People give you big business-smiles, and you wonder what

Who would you be without
the thought that you need
to make an impression?

they want. Companies have employees stand outside their chain stores to greet you as if they know you. Cashiers read your name off your credit card and say, "Thank you, Mrs. Smith."

When someone pretends to be interested in you, do you smile back and pretend to be flattered? Most people cheerily carry on with the playacting, and there's no problem unless you begin to think there's any real approval in this behavior. This isn't friendship—it *mimics* friendship to get people to do what someone wants. That kind of deception may sell insurance, but what happens when it enters the realms of friendship and your love life? Let's take a look.

MAKING YOURSELF MORE AGREEABLE

Winning people over by pretending to be interested in them is part of a bigger project: trying to become a more likeable person.

How do you react when you believe the thought that you can find love and approval by making yourself more likeable? If the person you are doesn't seem to be attracting enough interest, it seems natural to make some changes, to modify your appearance and your personality until you hit the right combination and become more appealing. Most people begin with the physical, trying out dozens of variations of outfits, hairdos, makeup, diets, walks, and facial expressions. This progresses to figuring out when to smile, when to make eye contact, when to laugh, when to talk, when to keep quiet, and what opinions to have.

A built-in part of developing a personality that's designed to please is constantly watching for signs that you're succeeding. This can be a stressful way to live. Anxiously focusing on the other person, checking for approval or disapproval, leaves nobody at home in yourself, nobody noticing your thoughts or taking responsibility for your feelings. This cuts you off from the source of real contentment. The outward focus also leaves unnoticed and unquestioned the inevitably painful thought that if you have to transform yourself to find love and approval, there must be something wrong with the way you are.

> I thought I had him convinced that I was intelligent, well-read, interesting, smart, even brilliant. I devoted our entire one-month relationship to this pursuit. He told me he didn't want to see me again! When I asked him why, he said that he was looking for someone less intense, someone more open, even someone simple, not so smart. After I got over the blow to my pride, I realized that the real me could have been a perfect match.

MINDING YOUR MANNERS

Manipulation often happens without anyone intending to do it or even noticing. For instance, in the excitement of new friendships or love affairs, you may find yourself bending your likes and dislikes to win the approval of other people (whether or not other people have expressed their own likes and dislikes). Do you find yourself saying yes when you mean no? ("Are you really sure it's okay?" "Oh yes, no problem, I'll sit in the backseat with your three wet golden retrievers.") When you start noticing it, you'll find that polite behavior is full of approval seeking disguised as consideration.

Politeness and tact are supposed to be about consideration for others. But notice how often they are really about trying to control the impression you make. When you say "Thank you," are you handing someone a token, or are you expressing real gratitude? When you're being polite, are you living your part or just playing it? The difference to notice here is the difference it makes to you.

For example, many people find it difficult to receive a kind remark or a gift. The focus on reciprocating right away, even with a thank-you, can keep you from fully receiving. Wanting to appear polite can prevent you from entering the state of gratitude where anxiety and separation disappear.

When you feel real gratitude, it shows without effort. Whether or not anybody notices is up to them. But if they do notice, they receive a much bigger gift—not small words and gestures, but gratitude itself. People become very open in the presence of gratitude. Soon they want to give you everything. Things get out of control, and love appears.

You can see this clearly with a hug. You don't experience the hug you're getting if you're trying to hug back. Trying to give back right away is refusing the gift. When you really receive it, you feel the arms around you, you feel the body, and you feel the love inside you. The receiving *is* the giving. It's the most genuine thing you can give back. That's what they wanted to give you in the first place.

TACT

Once you begin to notice your own approval seeking, the social niceties you find yourself engaged in become good opportunities for learning. Often tact means pretending not to notice when someone makes a mistake during his performance—for instance, when a colleague gets a famous name wrong while trying to impress you with his connections. Sometimes tact means simply trying to avoid offending someone. That's how people get involuntarily stuck together at social events. One person is talking about politics because she thinks that's what the other is interested in, and the other is trying to look interested. Both are bored, uncomfortable, and aware that they aren't doing well at their pretending. They are stuck because neither one questions the thought that it would give offense to say, "Enough about politics. Let's talk about something else." So, instead of discovering what they have in common, they struggle on, searching for potential rescuers out of the corners of their eyes.

Even good friends can fall victim to tact. Suppose you are playing your violin for your boyfriend, and he's pretending to like it in order to please you. As you watch him, he breaks character for a moment and his smile looks pained—that's his tactless lapse into honesty. Your expression changes as you notice his lapse, and that's your tactless lapse—letting him know that you noticed. But you both behave as if nothing happened. You struggle through to the end of your performance (you've been having a difficult time with the high notes), allowing your boyfriend to finish his performance of enjoying it. Each of you wants to support the other in the job of pretending.

Why bother with all this complicated pretending? There is no reason. You do it because neither of you has questioned the belief that your relationship depends on playacting and couldn't stand up to honesty. You walk on eggshells around each other because you don't even realize there's another option.

EXCUSE ME. I'M SORRY.

Like tact, apologies are often charades. Sometimes they're harmless charades, like when someone almost flattens you with a shopping cart and you say, "Excuse me." You don't want even strangers to lower their opinion of you. A friend of mine who went back to retrieve a magazine he'd left in a doctor's crowded waiting room made a speech excusing himself to everyone. He wanted them all to understand that he wasn't a used-magazine thief.

Full-time approval seeking means that instead of just living your life, you have to act it out. Waiting for a bus on a neighborhood street corner, you can't just wait for the bus. Every once in a while you have to step off the sidewalk and peer into the distance, doing a performance of someone waiting for a bus. Otherwise, one of the bystanders might think you're up to no good.

Exercise: Life Beyond Manners

Notice how often you defend yourself (with words, actions, the way you dress, your tone of voice) and how stressful that can be. What impression—what "you"—are you trying to hide or strengthen? Whom are you trying to convince? What is the story of "you" that you perpetuate or want to perpetuate? What "you" would you be without this story?

Notice when you make excuses, explain, or justify yourself (or do the same for others, tactfully helping them out by offering them an excuse). What do you experience when you defend, qualify, or explain even your very existence? What are you afraid we'll think or do if you remain silent and don't defend, justify, qualify, explain yourself, or tell us what *really* happened unless we ask? Make a list, then one by one ask yourself if each item on it is true.

> I'm afraid you'll think I'm rude, and then _____.
> I'm afraid you'll think I don't care about you, and
> then _____.
> I'm afraid you'll think I'm too _____, and then _____.

What do you believe about the above imaginary consequences? How do you react when you believe that thought? Who would you be without the thought?

What would happen if you moved and responded with less concern about what others will think? What if you let your actions speak for themselves? What would it be like to live your truth without excusing, defending, explaining, or justifying your thoughts or actions to others?

The following exercises are not about flouting good manners or changing your behavior. They are about helping you see what you may be hiding from yourself when you're intent on acting in a socially acceptable way: anxious thoughts that you don't really believe.

- Imagine leaving the table without a polite excuse, and notice what the excuse is designed to prevent. If you were to just get up and leave without any words, what do you think they would think of you?
- Imagine a situation in which you slightly inconvenience someone, perhaps by being late or wanting to borrow something. What if you were to simply apologize without explanation? Imagine yourself standing in front of that person without your explanation. Notice what impression your explanation would have been designed to prevent. What do you think would happen if someone were to form the very impression of you that you're afraid of? Do you really believe that thought?

When you say or do anything to please, get, keep, influence, or control anyone or anything, fear is the cause and pain is the result. Manipulation is separation, and separation is painful. Another person can love you totally in that moment, and you'd have no way of realizing it. If you act from fear, there's no way you can receive love, because you're trapped in a thought about what you have to do for love. Every stressful thought separates you from people.

But once you question your thoughts, you discover that you don't have to do anything for love. It was all an innocent misunderstanding. When you want to impress people and win their approval, you're like a child who says, "Look at me! Look at me!" It all comes down to a needy child. When you can love that child and embrace it yourself, the seeking is over.

Talking, Interrupting, and Listening

Most efforts to win love and admiration aren't coldly calculated—
it's not as if we do it on purpose. Flirtation, seduction, falling in
love, and the whole romantic realm take place in a dreamy,
trancelike state, alternating between hope and fear. One minute
you think you may be rejected; the next minute you're excited
about succeeding. In this state you hardly know what you're
doing, and you may hide from yourself how much you pretend
and manipulate.

The dreamlike state is most intense when people get close
to consummating their relationships, whether it's businesspeople
on the verge of making a deal, closing a sale, or getting hired for
a job, or lovers about to have sex for the first time. Everybody
wants to be in agreement and to gloss over their differences.

If this state of mind is stressful for you, you can begin to
wake up just by noticing what goes on in the ordinary chat that
surrounds it. Conversation is full of unintentional behavior aimed
at managing other people's impressions: flirtatious smiles, mean-
ingful looks, nods of agreement, and exaggerated reactions.

HOW DO YOU TALK WHEN
YOU'RE SEEKING APPROVAL?

Do you ever freeze when you're asked a simple question? What
are you afraid of? You're on the verge of putting your thoughts
and opinions out there in full view. You think you need to agree
with people to win their approval, but you're not sure what they
think yet, so you don't know what to say.

One solution is to avoid going first when giving your opinions. If you have to go first, you make your statements as mal-
leable as possible. Little words like *but* and *because* become your

best friends, since they let you do a 180-degree turn in the middle of a sentence. If you sense that you're saying the wrong thing, you can back right out of it in the same breath: "I loved *Lord of the Rings*" (noticing a flinch) "*but* it was much too long." The word *but* brings you back into agreement. "I love filet mignon" (noticing a look of vegetarian horror) "*although* I really prefer steamed vegetables." (According to a psychologist friend from Moscow, during the Soviet regime the word meaning "although" was the most important word in the Russian language.) Words like *because* can serve a similar, less drastic function. "I spent the weekend in Las Vegas" (startled look) "*because* my wife likes to gamble."

Another strategy is to clam up completely. Here's how that worked out for one woman:

> When I was about thirty, I was in a relationship with an older guy. He liked to drink a lot, cook, eat out, party, and make music with his friends. I was struggling to get a promotion at work and struggling with everything about myself. I spent most weekends at his house. In the morning we would get up and tend to the business of breakfast or just getting the day started. Except to discuss the details of these things, I wouldn't speak. I was trying to figure out what he wanted me to do or say so we could be together. I was frozen and couldn't do anything until I knew that my actions would yield the desired result. Eventually he asked me, "What's wrong with you? Why are you so catatonic?" I was furious.

Exercise: Interruption

A good way to become aware of the thoughts that fly by during a conversation is to watch yourself interrupting people. You probably notice when someone interrupts you in midsentence, but if you're the one doing it, it may not be so obvious.

STEP ONE.

Simply notice when you interrupt. Don't stop your interrupting; just notice it. Try this during a phone call or while chatting with your mother or a colleague at the office.

STEP TWO.

As you interrupt, silently say this to yourself: "I'm not letting you finish your sentence because _____" (and fill in the blank). This will hardly slow you down at all. Just watch, and let the blank fill itself in with what you usually hide from yourself in the blur of conversation.

Here are some examples of what various people have discovered:

"I'm not letting you finish your sentence because
   . . . I already know where you're going, and I have something more clever to say."
   . . . I might forget what I have to say and lose this great opportunity to impress you."
   . . . I already know where you're going, and I want to avoid that territory."
   . . . you aren't interesting enough to distract me from my scary thoughts."
   . . . you're having such a hard time expressing yourself, I'm going to rescue you by saying it better."
   . . . interrupting you is a natural expression of my enthusiasm."

When you've done this exercise enough times to recognize the top three thoughts that lead you to interrupt, ask yourself if they're true, and continue with how you react when you believe the thoughts, and who you would be without them. Then turn the thoughts around.

Exercise: Tuning Out

Instead of interrupting, you may find that you simply tune out while someone is talking to you, and from then on, you just pretend to listen. Try to notice the moment when you begin to listen to your own thoughts instead of the words of the other person. Then say this silently to yourself: "I've decided to attend to my thoughts instead of to what you're saying because _____." For example:

> ". . . I've heard this before, and I can safely go back to a more important project: nursing my worries."
>
> ". . . I can't afford to listen to this. If I don't pay attention to my own troubles, I may not survive the week."
>
> ". . . the people laughing over there are having more fun. I wonder if I can join them."

Find your favorite reasons for tuning out and bring them to inquiry. People say they "space out," whereas in reality they shift their attention to particular thoughts. Where do you go when you space out?

Exercise: Lunch Date

Make a lunch date with two or more lively friends. When you meet, after your usual greetings, let your friends do all the talking. Let yourself get totally involved with the conversation, but without joining in except to nod, smile, or look concerned when appropriate. If they ask you a question, answer briefly. During the conversation, you might say an occasional "I hear you" or "You could be right." Nothing more.

Notice the thoughts that would normally cause you to say something. Do you, or does the conversation, seem to suffer when you listen instead of talk? Be aware of the contribution you make just by listening. As you leave, make no mention of, or apology for, your quiet behavior (did anyone even notice?) and make a date to meet again soon.

A young man who always wanted to be admired told this story about how life showed him who he is without his approval seeking:

> I used to talk nonstop to entertain people so that they would admire me. When I went to China for the first time, I could only say a few words, very slowly, to allow the interpreters to keep up with me. I also had to work hard to make out what people were saying to me. To my amazement, everyone liked me, and I enjoyed the people I met just as much. I had always heard that China was a hard place to work, but I found the people extremely kind. It wasn't until I got back to the States and found myself talking less and getting more love that I realized that what had happened had nothing to do with China.

AN EXPERIMENT IN TRUE LISTENING

Spend a day listening to people. Just let their words in without superimposing your own thoughts. You can try out the idea that when people talk, they're finding their way toward what they really mean, and that the best way to help them is to just listen. Allow yourself to take in what they say without wondering what

their point is. Trust that when they stop talking you'll understand. When you want to finish a sentence for them—out loud
or in your mind—stop yourself.

It can be amazing to hear what gifts come out of people's
mouths when you allow them to complete their thoughts without
interruption. Sometimes you meet an entirely different person
(especially if it happens to be someone you're married to). You
may find that when you thought you were getting to know someone, you were just confirming your beliefs about who they are.
Some simple misunderstandings clear themselves up right away.
For example, a friend told me that his colleague always seemed
irritated at him. Then one day my friend let him finish what he
was trying to say, without prompting or interruption, and the colleague was so relieved that he told my friend, without a trace of
irritation, how much he enjoys working with him.

Your understanding of another person is limited by what you
think you already know. So when you just listen, the person you
meet won't match your preconception. The exciting thing is that
you usually meet someone much wiser and kinder than you
expected. You may also lose track of your ideas about who *you* are.
You become a true listener, an open and genuinely interested person. Maybe you too will be wiser and kinder than you thought you
were. It's not hard to be interested when people keep surprising
you and showing that they have more to offer than you expected.

When you listen literally, you may feel disoriented at first.
The identity you usually work so hard at upholding falls away.
You won't be the person who used to flip through her mental files
while someone was talking, waiting for a chance to break in and
impress them. That person turns out to be just another burden,
another obstacle to true meeting. In literal listening, someone you
didn't know you were meets someone you didn't know you knew.

Do You Really Need Approval? An Inquiry

It sometimes happens that once you start noticing your untrue thoughts about approval seeking, and the uncomfortable behavior that results from it, the approval seeking stops by itself. The thoughts unravel, and you are left to live your life in a much happier way. If that doesn't happen, and you still think you need the approval of a particular person, sit down and write out an inquiry. Ask yourself the four questions and find some turnarounds, as the young woman did in the example below.

I need my father's approval.

Is that true?

Yes, I need him to respect and appreciate what I do.

Can I absolutely know that it's true?

No, but I still think I need his approval.

How do I react when I think I need his approval? How do I treat him when I believe that thought?

First, I try to impress him with my accomplishments. I mention celebrities I've met through my new job. I invite him for a drive in my new car. I try to appear stylish and confident. Then I feel hurt and angry because it doesn't seem to be impressing him. I feel frustrated that he's never heard of the celebrities. In the car, he asks where he's supposed to put his legs, and I get annoyed. He looks at my new piercing and says, "What's that on your nose?" I give him the cold treatment. I call him ignorant when he says he thought Paris Hilton was a hotel. I pretend to look down on him when really I'm afraid he'll say something devastating.

Does this thought bring me closer to my father or separate me from him?

It makes me feel very separate. I get more and more aloof to hide how hurt I am. It's like we live in different worlds, separated by a huge generation gap.

Who would I be without the thought that I need his approval? Who would I be in his presence if I couldn't think that thought?

It would be so different. It would be a huge relief. I don't see myself talking about work so much. I begin to wonder about him—I don't know much about my dad these days. Without that thought, when I think about the cutting remarks he makes, I see they aren't meant to be cutting. It's him trying to be funny, trying to connect with me and not knowing how. I feel close to him again.

"I need my father's approval"—turn it around.

I need *my* approval.

Is that as true as or truer than the original statement?

Yes, absolutely. The truth is that *I'm* not comfortable with the things I try to impress my father with. The people my company represents are often jerks, and I'm supposed to treat them like royalty. And I don't really like the clothes I wear for the job. When I think I need my approval, I can see some changes that would give me my approval right away. I don't have to bend over as far as I do at work. I could drop certain clients, wear different clothes—the list goes on, and none of it is hard.

Is there another turnaround?

I need to approve of my father.

Is that as true or truer?

Yes. It would feel good to let him know what I've been discovering. I can see how I've punished him with my defensiveness, and I'd like to tell him about that and give him a big kiss. I'd like to tell him that some of his jokes are really funny, and that I've pretended to be mad instead because laughing would have rewarded him for disapproving of me. I'd much rather just laugh.

Is there another turnaround?

I *don't* need my father's approval.

Is that as true or truer?

It is; I can see that. The fact is that when I have my own approval, I'm happy, and I don't need anyone else's. Their approval is just icing on the cake. It's extra, and it's not necessary for me to be happy. Anyway, if my dad approved of me for things I don't like about myself, I wouldn't believe him. He wouldn't be doing me any favors. He respects my ability to solve my own problems. I know that because when he sees me struggling, he doesn't try to rescue me. What it comes down to is that I don't need his approval because I already have it. As I look at it now, I have a lot of proof of that.

Exercise: The Ultimate Approval Giver

When you believe you need the approval of a particular person, this exercise is another simple way to inquire.

Think of a person (living or dead) whose approval would mean a lot to you; the person could be a teacher, mentor, boss, mother, father, son, daughter, an expert in your field, or just a crabby aunt. Now ask yourself what you would want that person to say about you, and write down the words that would express the approval you've been seeking. This is your chance to have him or her say exactly what you want to hear. Examples:

> Crabby aunt: "I like the life you've created. It's interesting and worthwhile."
>
> Former third-grade teacher: "I was completely wrong about you. You didn't turn out to be a ne'er-do-well after all."
>
> Mahatma Gandhi: "You're really not as selfish as you think you are."
>
> Your son: "You're a wonderful mom."
>
> The boss: "I deeply appreciate your work."
>
> God: "You're okay. I'm glad I made you."

Now read over what you've written and ask yourself if you agree with what these people say. Do you agree with your crabby aunt? (In real life, of course, she probably wouldn't say anything nice.) The point is, do *you* think you have an interesting and worthwhile life? If you agree, notice how it feels to recognize yourself in this way, to already have the approval that you wanted from your aunt. Now notice the effect of subtracting that "need" when you think of your aunt or imagine spending time with her.

When you do this exercise, you may come across a statement that you don't completely agree with. For example, you may not appreciate your work quite so much as your imagined boss does. If that happens, ask yourself what *you* can do to feel better about your work—for *your* approval.

I'm a cameraman who had the rare opportunity to work on a film crew with a famous director. During breaks in the filming I would hover around the director hoping to get some praise for my work (I knew he was watching it on a video monitor). I awkwardly stood around while the director was busy working with the actors. On one occasion he asked me if I wanted something. I shook my head and went back to work frustrated and ashamed of myself for being so needy. I was also embarrassed to notice how pleased I was that he knew my name.

That night I went over the scene in my mind and asked myself what I wanted to hear from the director. The answer appeared immediately: "You did nice work on the close-ups." At the same time I realized that my pans and tilts could have been smoother. I noticed that my anxiety had completely disappeared.

The next day's shoot was a new experience. I gave myself the small corrections I needed during filming, and when I saw the director relaxing with some other crew members, I joined in with ease. I had no thought that I needed his praise. Without my agenda, I began to notice for myself and appreciate what made this director unusual. He has asked for me on several shoots since that time, and I have never wanted more than the occasional smile he gives me.

We all do emotional gymnastics
to be seen as wonderful or
funny—just to get what we
already have. And because
we're doing the gymnastics, we
don't see that we already have it.

Who Would You Be Without the Thought That You Need to Seek Approval?

You might be someone who just lives your life and lets people form whatever impressions they want to form—of you and of everyone else. That's what they're all doing anyway. And if that seems like too big a leap, or if you think it would leave you without a reason to get out of bed in the morning, try the following exercise. It allows you to take a small step in your imagination that can make a big difference in your life.

Thought Experiment: A Cup of Tea

Think of someone you want to impress

or

whose love you want

or

who you're afraid of displeasing

or

who you think has power over you.

Imagine having a cup of tea with this person. Imagine that during this time you don't make the slightest attempt to influence her mental life. Imagine that all you want is to let her have her thoughts, her tea, her experience.

Thoroughly imagine yourself in that scene. What does it feel like to sit in the presence of that person in this way? What do you notice about how it feels to be you? What do you notice about the other person?

Here's an example from a friend of how the "cup of tea" experiment was used to look at a work relationship:

Before starting on a new article for the magazine I write for, I usually have to go to New York and sell the idea to my editor. I imagined having a cup of tea with her.

The first thing I noticed is that it felt very restful. I could see how much more I'd find out about this person, who has been my editor for several years. I saw that usually I only get glimpses of her out of the corner of my eye because my attention is on the pitch I'm making to get an assignment— trying to appear brilliant enough to convince her that my idea would be successful. Even when I succeed, I leave feeling exhausted and with less enthusiasm for my project. I discovered that finding out more about her would be interesting and I would enjoy her company. When I imagined pitching my story without trying to influence her mental life, I saw that I was actually describing it to myself, only I could hear it better in her presence. The idea grew and changed as I told it; I liked it better and left it up to her to like it or not. I felt open to her suggestions and saw that if the two of us could "have tea" in this way, without my trying to influence her mental life, good ideas might naturally float to the surface and we could have a lot of fun exploring them.

I wondered why I never do have a literal cup of tea with my editor. After doing the exercise I remembered that early on she had invited me to see her garden and that I had declined because I was afraid of my own motives; if I said yes I thought I might have been pretending to be interested in her and her garden in order to get work. I was too worried about this to even ask myself if I liked her. How silly! Doing the Cup of Tea experiment, I realized that I really did like her and felt open to her invitation. We haven't had tea yet, but now we sometimes have dinner together. I have found a friend, and my articles for the magazine have improved.

How do you react when you think that you need people's love? Do you become a slave for their approval? Do you live an inauthentic life because you can't bear the thought that they might disapprove of you? Do you try to figure out how they would like you to be, and then try to become that, like a chameleon? In fact, you can never really get their love this way. You try to turn into someone you aren't, and then when they say "I love you," you can't believe it, because they're loving a façade. They're loving someone who doesn't even exist, the person you're pretending to be. It's difficult to seek other people's love. It's deadly. In seeking it, you lose what is genuine. This is the prison we create for ourselves as we try to get the love we already have.

4

FALLING IN LOVE

❧

The search for approval from friends, associates, and family members is a full-time job with no vacations. At its center lies the search for ultimate approval, the search that all the songs are about, for the person who will look at us and say, "You're the one." We call this "falling in love." In this chapter we'll look at falling in love and becoming a couple, and we'll see who is really "the one."

Falling in love is usually understood completely backward, like so many other important things. There's no mystery to falling in love. We have fallen out of the awareness of love and are ecstatic when we find our way back, misunderstanding how we did it. Remember the little girl doing flips in the corner of the playground? She has the key. Look at her face, lit up with the excitement of perfection. She's overjoyed just to be there with her legs and arms to play with. There is absolutely nothing more that she wants or needs, and she's too absorbed in the moment to realize it. The flip she does is an expression of love itself. When she does the flip again, looking to see if she can win applause, she shifts her focus outward and cuts herself off from love. But love doesn't go anywhere; she just loses her awareness of it. Later in life, people call experiences like this "falling out of love" and think that they're about the other person.

The little girl is innocently misdirected. She begins to think that the way back to her happiness—to a perfect moment— depends on the reaction of the other kids. Even though the awareness of love is always available, years might pass before she has it again, years she devotes to searching for love and approval outside herself.

When you're constantly trying to be likeable, you leave no gaps in your life in which you can just breathe and notice what you already have, no chance to experience the unlimited options that those gaps are filled with. Even after you've attracted admirers and supporters, you're still busy seeking results. You have to make sure that your friends do all the things friends are supposed to do—invite you to parties, send work your way, console you when you feel depressed. And it's never enough. You're constantly on the lookout for any evidence that you're not approved of or adored.

"Falling in love" is a powerful experience. If you look back, you may remember it as a moment when you stopped seeking. You stopped because you thought you'd found what you were looking for. Your mind was no longer filled with the effort, the desperation, of seeking. What you found is what you had in the corner of the playground and never really lost. But now you think it's coming from another person, someone who is "the one."

Many people fall in love for the first time as teenagers. By that time the simple playground joy has vanished (actually *you* left *it*, but that's not how it seems). Dark thoughts appear—anxiety about how you're not all right and how no one can ever love you. Then the miracle happens: Suddenly there is someone to love, and you can stop searching. Maybe it's a boy in your chemistry class or a singer you saw at a rock concert. Maybe it's a movie star or your best friend's new girlfriend. With this kind of love you're just as happy when there's no hope of return. You don't mind if a kiss is completely out of the question because you have braces on your teeth, or because you would never betray your friend, or because there is no possibility of meeting the rock star. These may be the very reasons that you let yourself love completely.

When you look back on that first crush, it's possible to see that the girl you adored had nothing to do with it. Years later you can run into her again, stare at her all you want, and not have a clue what you saw there. You would have done anything to marry her, and now you're grateful that she never noticed you.

If the love isn't coming from the other person, whom does that leave? There's only one person left: you. *You* gave yourself the experience. The blissful feeling was not caused by how wonderful or sexy your best friend's girlfriend was. It was you who felt the wonder and the excitement. Someone held up a mirror and showed you your heart.

There are those who say that a crush is a delusion, that it wasn't real because it all came from you. Another way to look at it is that the crush was as real as any experience you'll ever have: you just made a mistake about where the joy was coming from. The source wasn't the brown-eyed girl or Leonardo DiCaprio; it was your own long-lost capacity to experience pure joy. When you had the crush, you found your way back to the child doing flips just for herself. That's the one you abandoned in order to seek an identity that you thought others would recognize. What we may think of as "first love" really takes us back to love itself, which is what we are to begin with.

You find other ways to fall in love when you get older. As you leave your teens, the worst of your awkwardness diminishes; your approval-getting skills get better with practice. After many trials, you may find someone who approves of you so much that they tell you, "You're the one." You like that. You like to be approved of that much. And maybe you approve of them for other reasons as well (and maybe not, and even that won't necessarily stop you).

Since you've been approved of, you can ease up for a while: there's much less straining to please and charm. Without your efforts getting in the way, love just flows. You bask in the happiness of it. Sometimes it seems like there's enough love to include everyone and everything you meet. Again, you'll probably think it's all about him, the one who thinks you're the one. But the happiness is really you returning to yourself. Love was there all along; only your painful thoughts obscured it.

How long does that joy last? Grownup love is like the crush—it lasts only until painful thoughts cover it over. "What if she doesn't really love me?" "He doesn't listen." "She shouldn't have flirted with that guy." Any one of these thoughts will destroy your happiness. And one way or another, that happiness will have to vanish as long as you believe the thought that love—the joy you stumbled into—depends on the other person.

Most people believe that having love in their lives and escaping loneliness depends on finding some special person. This is an ancient belief, and it takes courage to question it. But if you do, you're in for a big surprise: You can feel love either with or without someone in your arms. And no, that doesn't mean that you won't have a partner. Why would it? When *with* and *without* are equal, you notice that both are good: life allows all flavors.

The old song asks, "Why do fools fall in love?" Actually, only fools *don't* fall in love. Only a fool would believe the lonely, stressful thoughts that tell him that anything could separate him from another human being, or from the rest of the human race, or from birds, trees, pavement, and sky.

Don't believe me. Ask yourself. Try the next exercise.

Exercise: Who Would You Be Without the Thought That Your Happiness Depends on Someone Else?

If you are feeling your way into this question, here's an exercise that may help you answer it.

First of all, remind yourself what love means to you. What *is* the experience of love for you?

To locate this experience, be still, close your eyes, and remember a particular moment when you experienced love. Remember how it felt in your body. Perhaps it was a moment when you were lying in someone's arms, or you were diving off a board, or you were watching a sleeping child, or you may even have been alone and not doing anything out of the ordinary.

When you find the moment that love appeared, try something you may not have done before. Turn your focus inward and relive the sensations of it. Instead of focusing on the person or thing that you believe brought you your experience of love, notice what happened inside you. Focus on what you felt. Simply live in that experience for a while, so that you know what it is.

Write down a few words that express the experience. Notice what it takes for you to feel like that again, right now or in any moment.

Here's what one woman found when she did the experiment:

I grew up with parents who seemed to want a certain kind of daughter: quiet, unassuming, talented but modest, respectful, smart but humble. I thought that in order to get their love and approval I needed to be that person.

It was a hard game to play, but I learned the rules well, and it looked like I was the good daughter they wanted. I learned that to get people to like me, I had to figure out what they wanted and pretend to be that person. This seemed to be very effective, especially once I started to attract the opposite sex.

From age fifteen to twenty-five, I managed to make many boys and men fall in love with "me." It was always dramatic and interesting, but I personally never felt very involved. Once I got his attention, I'd complain that he didn't love the real me, and I'd move on.

One man broke the pattern. He didn't respond to the probes I designed to find out what he wanted me to be; he didn't even seem to notice them. He just watched and listened to me. I knew he was falling for me, but I couldn't figure out his angle. I didn't know how to act or who to be. When I burst into tears at a fancy restaurant, he took me out to the car and held me while I cried. He didn't even try to make me explain. (Of course, that would have been impossible at the time.)

One night, our plan was for me to go to his apartment for dinner and spend the night. He called that evening to say that he'd had an exhausting day at work. He wanted to call it an early night and go to bed, and he'd see me tomorrow. I felt furious and rejected, but I said, "No problem. I'm tired too." Then I got all dressed up and went out to a dance club with every intention of attracting some other guy to even the score. But when I got to the club, I just sat there and began to question what had happened. "He rejected me." "He's playing games with me." I saw that I didn't really believe this. I realized that I was the one playing a game and that I didn't have to. I didn't have to win. Relief flooded my whole body, and the music began to move right through me. I found myself leaping onto the dance floor alone, literally dancing for joy. I danced for hours, crying, sweating, and laughing.

This is the experience of love that I relived when I did the experiment. When I look inside myself, this is my experience of love. I can stop struggling. I can stop being scared. I can just be.

Love Story

As we have seen, falling in love feels wonderful. It feels so good that you want to keep it forever by becoming a couple. You're still taking a break from approval seeking and all the painful thoughts that go with it. You're also having a lot of sex—one of the few ways most people give themselves some relief from their thoughts. And then love seems to wear off. Why do we have that impression?

Here's the story of a quiet, home-loving woman who is powerfully attracted to an outdoorsy NASCAR fan. They meet at work, where she is the librarian. While they date, she pretends to enjoy watching stock-car races, taking part in paint-gun battles in the woods, and going to the victory parties afterward. He notices the signs of strain in her but thinks that she is what she presents herself to be—a more sensitive version of himself. He, in turn, pretends that he likes Japanese food, and also that he wants to stay home and watch movies with her instead of going out to sports bars with his friends. She thinks that he is a more outgoing version of herself. They fall in love and move in together.

High on feelings of acceptance and approval, and lacking any way of understanding what has happened to them, the lovers continue to think that their façades have brought them love. But, though they may be minimally aware of this, they are also feeling doubt and fear. Neither of them can really believe it when the other says, "I love you." The thought they keep to themselves is: "He [she] loves what I'm pretending to be; I doubt that he could love what I really am." (If they've been around the block a few times, they're also hiding this thought: "I love what he's pretending to be; I'm not sure how I feel about who he really is.") These doubtful thoughts don't cause too much trouble at first, because the lovers are basking in the blissful feelings that they link to the other person.

What spoils the love fest is that, as time passes, the effort of maintaining their façades takes its toll, and those hidden doubts appear more often. One day she gets honest and admits that she'd rather stay home for the weekend than go to the Daytona 500. He feels confused and let down (though, for his part, he's been living in fear that one of his friends will see him coming out of the library). The recriminations begin.

She says, "You lied to me. You said you liked to stay home in the evenings and have time for our relationship." Or, "You used to like staying home with me, you've changed, you don't love me anymore."

He says, "You lied to *me*. You said you loved the things I love and wanted to be with me no matter what."

Deep inside themselves, each of the lovers knows that the other is right, but they think they would lose ground if they admitted it instead of attacking back. They would love to stop the pretending, but they stick to the beliefs that seemed to have worked so far. So, staying in the roles that they've created (by now, they no longer realize that these are roles), they experience disappointment and anger.

The lovers may now think they don't even like each other, and they may break up without ever truly meeting the person they've been living with. They have gone directly from their original façades to operating angry "me" puppets, each of them feeling betrayed by the other. To get to this kind of impasse, couples always pass up chances to reverse directions. For example, she could say, "You're right, honey, I tried to like NASCAR, but I hated it. I had to wear earplugs. I did that to make you love me. I wanted you to accept me and find me exciting. Did it work?"

"What!"

"I admit it, I lied. I pretended to like NASCAR because I was afraid you wouldn't love me if I didn't. Is that true? Would you love me anyway?"

Now he's at a fork in the road: Will he admit that he lied about liking sushi, or will he accuse her of being a phony and go back to operating his angry "me" puppet? She's taken the risk of telling the truth. If he joins her and takes the risk too, revealing his own doubts and fears, they've changed direction and are moving toward asking and finding what's really true for them. They might have something genuine and wonderful going: the beginning of honest relationships with themselves, and—who knows?—maybe even with each other.

How can you know that a particular relationship is good or not? When you are out of sync with goodness, you know it: You aren't happy. And if a relationship is anything less than good, you need to question your thoughts. It's your responsibility to find your own way back to a relationship with yourself that makes sense.

When you have that sweet relationship with yourself, your partner is an added pleasure. It's over-the-top grace.

Romantic love is the story of how you need another person to complete you. It's an absolutely insane story. My experience is that I need no one to complete me. As soon as I realize that, everyone completes me.

5

PERSONALITIES DON'T LOVE—THEY WANT SOMETHING

⚜

Many couples stay together despite the disappointment and resentment that arise when they drop their façades. They still want something from each other, and they think they can get it. Two things they often want are comfort and security. Each looks at the other and thinks, "You aren't the person you pretended to be when we met, but *if you give me what I want,* I'll stay with you and go on calling it love." They believe that comfort and security are a good compensation for their disappointment. And they rationalize settling for them as a realistic and inevitable thing. Their thinking includes such painful beliefs as "Love never lasts," "This is all I deserve," and "Being with someone I don't love is better than being alone."

How comfortable is settling, really? In cozy arrangements the partners think they've given up passion for comfort because comfort is as good as it gets. They expect a large, reliable supply of security to make up for their lost passion. If their partner fails to deliver on what is usually a long list of security or comfort items, the anger can be explosive.

Suppose she has been trying her best to give him what he wants, often pretending that what he wants is also what she wants. And sometimes she knows very well that she doesn't really want to do these things. She tells herself that she's sacrificing her happiness, her life, to please him, make him happy, and have his love. Then she does one thing wrong, and he gets angry. Her resentment boils up, and there's a huge self-righteous explosion. It turns out that a lot of anger lay hidden under the coziness. Those angry "me" puppets come onto the stage again, and the original resentments reappear. "You lied to me when we were getting together, you've changed, you're not the man [woman] I married, you don't love me."

Is It Love When It Instantly Turns to Anger?

You feel entitled to be angry. After all, you've really put yourself out, you've opened up and made yourself vulnerable. You feel entitled to have your partner want what you want him to want.

The reality is that he doesn't. He just continues to want what *he* wants. He can't change his wants to suit you. Can *you* change *your* wants to suit anyone? Can *you* make yourself want something you don't want? Well, he's just like you.

We use our beauty, our cleverness, our charm to capture someone for a partnership, as if he were an animal. And then when he wants to get out of the cage, we're furious. That doesn't sound very caring to me. It's not self-love. I want my husband to want what he wants. And I also notice that I don't have a choice. That's self-love. He does what he does, and I love that. That's what I want, because when I'm at war with reality, it hurts.

The Oatmeal Man

The first time a certain young man slept over at his girlfriend's apartment, she served him her favorite breakfast: oatmeal. He didn't mention that he hated oatmeal, because he didn't want any disagreement between them, especially after they'd just had sex. He didn't question the thought that telling her the truth would displease her.

After they got married, she often served him oatmeal, and he continued to eat it. He thought that if he admitted his loathing for oatmeal now, he would displease her even more, since it would reveal that he'd been dishonest for a long time. He would rather eat oatmeal than face what he believed his wife would think of him if he told her the truth. And oatmeal is what he's still eating for breakfast, twenty-three years later.

Is there any oatmeal in your life? What do you do for love that you wouldn't do otherwise? I asked some friends this question, and one of them sent the following list:

> I ironed his shirts.
> I made nice dinners and pretended that I enjoyed doing it.
> I pretended I couldn't be hurt by anything he said.
> I pretended to be more hurt than I was by what he said.
> I pretended I always cared about what he said.
> I'm a night person, and I forced myself to become a
>   morning person.
> I cut my hair really, really short one time.
> I distanced myself from my family in order to show him
>   that I put him first.
> I tried to stop grieving my mother's death.
> I chose a career that didn't interest me.
> I wore uncomfortable underwear.

Make your own list of things you do for love that you wouldn't do otherwise. Then imagine reading each item to your partner and asking, "Has it worked? Is this what you love?"

"If You Love Me, You'll Do What I Want"—Is It True?

Horses grazing in a field unthinkingly stand head to tail, flicking the flies from each other's faces. At night, they sleep standing up, resting their heads on each other's shoulders. This is what peaceful reciprocation looks like. But "civilized" people have learned how to use reciprocation to torture each other. All it takes is the belief that if I do something for you, you owe me something in return. If I give you my love, you'd better give me yours, or something of equal value.

What happens if you don't reciprocate? I take back my love and approval, and I give you resentment instead. The rules of each relationship dictate all the things you have to do or not do to avoid resentment. These rules aren't written down or even spoken. You find out what they are by breaking them. When you see that I'm angry, you know you've broken a rule. You did something you shouldn't have, you came home too late or too early, you forgot to do or say something. Perhaps you should ask what you did wrong, but watch out: One of the rules may be that you're supposed to know without asking.

And, of course, you find out about *your* rules for *my* behavior using the same method. How do you know when I broke a rule? When you get angry at me.

In any case, if you do your best to figure out all the rules and obey them, do you get my love? No. You get to tiptoe around me, so that you can minimize my anger and continue the relationship.

Love seems to have disappeared. Where did it go? You can find out by questioning the thought "If you love me, you'll do what I want."

This is a thought most people have believed for as long as they can remember. The child expects his playmate to want to play the games *he* wants to play. If not, there's a big fight, and they both stomp off to find an adult to complain to: "He's not my friend anymore!" The belief that a friend is someone who will do what you want is already fully active in this child. He learned it from his parents, who told him they loved him and rewarded him with praise when he obeyed them, and punished him when he didn't. His parents never questioned the thought that obedience is an expression of love, so why would he?

Unquestioned thoughts about needs and wants launched the quest for love and approval to begin with. It's no surprise that after we win someone over, those same thoughts arise again. We haven't known how to question what we want from love. We haven't known how to question what we believe. We don't know that we can simply love, and that we can simply ask for what we want, with no strings attached.

Is It True?

This book could have been called *The Two Major Universal Whoppers About Love*. We looked at one of the whoppers in the chapter about approval seeking: "I need to win people over to make them like me" (also known as "I can manipulate your love and approval"). Now we've come to the other one: "If you love me, you'll do what I want." It *seems* reasonable—so reasonable that we've built an entire civilization on it. How can it be wrong? Let's stop and question it.

The following inquiry is one woman's attempt to be as thorough as possible. As you read it, substitute your own "you"—the person who you think doesn't love you because he or she doesn't do what you want—and see where you go.

"If you love me, you'll do what I want"—is it true?

It seems to be.

Can I absolutely know that it's true? What's the reality of it?

No, I can't absolutely know that that's true. The reality of it is that sometimes you don't do what I want.

How do I react when I believe the thought "If you love me, you'll do what I want"?

I assess everything you do for me and everything I do for you in terms of its exchange value. I keep a score sheet on our relationship to measure how much love you are giving me. I make lists of demands that I present to you in an aggrieved manner, saying or implying that I'll love you only if you deliver on my list. And I make other lists of what you would do if you really loved me. I present these to you angrily or use them internally as proof that you don't love or appreciate me. I withdraw from you, using your infractions, your failure to deliver, as my reason for the separation I inflict. I withhold sex. I don't give you what I secretly want to give you, and I feel a lot of shame and guilt about that, and then I hate myself and begin to overeat, I smoke and drink too much, and I justify my actions by blaming you for being so unfair. I get angry at you when I feel lonely or empty, thinking that if only you had done what I wanted, I wouldn't have to feel this way. I usually end up thinking that you don't love me.

Who would I be if I didn't believe the thought "If you love me, you'll do what I want"? What if that thought just passed through my mind like air?

I would look at you without keeping score. I wouldn't concern myself with whether something you've done means that you love me or not. If you didn't do what I want, it would be fine with me. I would understand why you didn't do it and why that was right for you in that moment, and if I didn't understand, I could ask you. I wouldn't take it personally. I would remain calm and happy. If what I wanted you to do for me was something I could do myself, I would simply do it. Without the thought "If you loved me, you'd do what I want," I would come back to myself. I would notice that I love you, and then continue with my own activities. It would be like not having you in my life except as someone I love and care about. I would be a much calmer and happier person. I would be grateful for you. I would like myself more.

Turn the thought around.

"If you love me, you *won't* do what I want." Yes, I can see how that is truer. Here are three examples of how my life has actually been better because you haven't done what I want. One: I remember the time I wanted to buy that stock and you said that it wasn't a good idea. You stuck to it, and the stock dumped, and we bought the

Prius with the money we would have lost. Thank you for not caving in to me. I love our Prius! A second example: I wanted you to go to an Indian restaurant with my friends, and you were absolutely clear in your refusal. I respect that. I respect that you didn't come along with us out of a feeling that you had to please me. You took care of your stomach, your time, and your integrity. Three: I flew to Las Vegas to see our grandchildren, and I really wanted you to go with me. You chose not to go on this particular weekend because you wanted to stay home and enjoy your solitude. I so much appreciated that you missed the busyness and raucousness of the life I shared with our children and grandchildren that weekend, the shopping for the twins, the wild noise in the kitchen, the constant laughter, food, and music. I loved thinking of you in your solitude, reading, working, taking long baths, communing quietly with your beautiful self, and living the life that we enjoy so much when we're together. I respect you for living out your own integrity, and our children do too, and they learn so much from your steadiness. I love how generous you are to yourself, to them, and to me, and how solid you are when you know to do or not to do something, and how you stick to it no matter what anyone says, including me.

Is there another turnaround?

"If I love myself, I'll do what I want." Yes. I sometimes sense a voice inside me that is telling me what's good, and I ignore it and don't listen, even the second or third time around. Sometimes I don't do what I know to do. I notice I sometimes ignore even the simplest inner direction. I want to call the children just to hear their voices, and sometimes I put it off, and I cheat myself out of such pleasure when I don't make the call.

Another turnaround?

"If I love you, I'll do what you want." Yes, I can see that. If I love you, I'll do what you want when that feels honest and right for me. When this is where I'm at, we both agree, and it's so simple, and it costs me nothing to hear you and to be there for you when you need me. Actually, that's what I want. When I let go of winning and losing, it's simple to give you what I really want to give you, and I am the one who benefits. I have realized that giving to you is giving happiness to myself. Also, when I give you what you want—for instance, when I go to places you want to go to, even when I think I'm not interested—I discover a lot about you and me. There is so much of your life that I haven't discovered, simply because I have predetermined that I wouldn't like it. Maybe it will be fascinating to do what I have rejected, just to see what's on the other side of doing it. Often when I do what you want, my life is more interesting. I learn a lot by listening to you with an open mind.

If love includes any or all of these turnarounds—"If you love me, you won't do what I want," "If I love myself, I'll do what I want," "If I love you, I'll do what you want"—what does that tell you? That you can happily unhook love from want and begin to live the experience of freedom.

Remember the man who moved in with the librarian at the end of the last chapter? When we left him, he was shocked to discover that she didn't like NASCAR and didn't want go to any more races with him. What if he realized that love has nothing to do with her doing what he wants? How might their life go on?

"Bye, I'm off to the races. Do you want to have dinner with me afterward—ribs at Houston's?"

"No thanks, honey. I love that you invited me, and I'm going to my poetry workshop."

"Okay. You do look happy there with your book and the cat."

"You look happy too. Have fun. I'll see you later."

Honest Communication

Knowing the difference between loving someone and wanting him to do what you want doesn't mean that you can't ask for what you want. You can, knowing that his answer has nothing to do with his love for you. You'll discover that asking is much easier when it's free of hidden agendas. And when he realizes that whatever he answers is fine with you, an amazing intimacy can open for you both.

Exercise: An Honest No

Honest communication begins with you communicating with yourself. It means responding with what is true for you, regardless of how someone may react to your answer. First you have to discover what is really true for you. A dishonest yes is a no to yourself.

Try this exercise. Imagine simply saying no when you feel torn by a request. Look at what you think would happen, write down the fearful thoughts that arise, and question them, especially the ones that sound like "If I say no, he won't love me" or "If I say no, she'll think I don't love her."

For example, your teenage daughter wants to borrow the car to go to a late-night party on a rainy night. She says that this party means everything to her. She says that she'll hate you forever if you don't give her the car. When you hesitate, what are you thinking? Now put these thoughts up against inquiry. "'She'll hate me if I say no'—is it true? How do I react when I believe that thought? Who would I be without the thought? What's the turnaround?"

Or your best friend asks if he can leave his dog in your tiny apartment while he goes to Hawaii for three weeks. Or your boyfriend wants to have sex with you, and you don't feel like it. Find your own divided moment and inquire. Realize that a no to them may mean a yes to you. And notice that it's possible to love without condition, even when your answer is no.

People ask for many things. Once you discover that your honest answer is no, communicating it is simple when you communicate your love at the same time. The no is one part of your answer, and the acknowledgment of your love is the other part. Here are some examples of how to express your honest no to these requests and still let people know that you hear them and respect that they're asking for what they want. Find out which words seem the most caring, natural, and true for you. Try these, and see how it feels to stay within your own integrity.

Thank you for asking, and no.
I understand, and no.
You could be right, and no.
I care about you, and no.
I can see that it works for you, and no.
I want to please you, and no.

I'm frightened to say no to you, please support me, and the
answer is no for now.

I don't know yet. Please ask me later.

Just Asking

If you're not a clear communicator, you may live your life unloved
and misunderstood, not ever realizing that if you just said what
you wanted, your whole world would change. Remember that the
first step in clear communication is communicating with yourself.

Imagine that there's something you want and you're having
trouble asking for it. You're hoping to get it from your partner, or
resenting him because you're not getting it, or trying to manipulate him by dropping hints or looking victimized and trying to
make him feel guilty, all the while feeling unloved. Now imagine
just asking for what you want, and write down the fearful thoughts
about possible consequences. "I want to spend Thanksgiving
vacation by myself this year and go on a yoga retreat. If I told my
husband, he might . . ." "I want my wife to be more affectionate
with me. If I asked her to touch me more, she might . . ." Now
question these thoughts. "'If I asked her, she would reject me'—is
that true? Can I absolutely know that it's true? How do I react
when I believe that thought? Who would I be without the
thought? What's the turnaround?"

Notice that once you have separated love from want, simply asking becomes much easier. But you have to ask. People
can't second-guess our desires; they aren't psychic on cue.

Practice just asking. Ask three people for something today.
Ask without being kind, manipulative, or careful. Ask simply and
clearly, without justifying your request. Notice the fear and also

the relief that may surface as you do this. Who would you be if you just asked for what you want straight up, rather than resenting that you didn't get what you didn't ask for?

Just Asking *You*

When you ask for what you want, it's important to realize that others may not always be able or willing (or, in some cases, dishonest enough) to accommodate your request. In that case, ask someone else, or turn it around and ask *you*. Give yourself what it is that you think you want. If everyone says no, who's left? Obviously, you're the one you've been waiting for.

Maybe you want someone to be more honest with you, talk to you, not talk to you so much, be your friend, leave you alone, not be so nice all the time. Can you give any of those things to yourself? Maybe you want a hug. What do you think a hug would give you? Feel that, and give it to yourself. If that doesn't work, ask someone directly, and if they say no and you still want the hug, ask someone else, and someone else, until you get it. Who is stopping you but you?

You may find that what you really want to ask for is love. If so, notice the impulse to trade something else for love. What would happen if you simply stopped the bartering and allowed yourself to feel love instead? For example, suppose you feel unloved by your partner, who doesn't seem to be paying attention to you. Suddenly you have an impulse to buy him a gift or do something "generous" for him. If you look more carefully, you may notice that you're trying to give the gift in exchange for some care and attention.

Suppose you give yourself the care and attention instead. Naturally, this means questioning the thought that's causing you pain. In this case, the thought may be "He's not paying attention to me, and that means that he doesn't love me." Is that true? Can you absolutely know that it's true? How do you react when you believe that thought? Who would you be without it? How would you turn the thought around?

After you finish the inquiry, see if you still want to buy him the gift. Maybe you do, and it's not in exchange for anything. One way to tell love from bartering is that when you give any-one a gift out of love you give the pleasure to yourself.

The voice within is what I'm married to. All marriage is a metaphor for that marriage. My lover is the place inside me where an honest yes or no comes from. That's my true partner. It's always there. And to tell you yes when my integrity says no is to divorce that partner.

THE RELATIONSHIP
WORKSHOP

⚭

As we have seen, there are two basic misconceptions about love: first, that you have to manipulate others to get it, and second, that love is about getting what you want. You may have discovered, with a little inquiry, that neither of these thoughts is true for you. It's obvious why relationships built on such foundations are difficult. And it's easy to see how you can have a happy relationship if you stay true to yourself.

So how do you stay true to yourself? The first step is to remember that your most intimate relationship is the one you have with your thoughts. This is the case whether you've been married for twenty years with six children, or you're single and dating, or you're divorced, lovelorn, solitary, or any combination of these. An open heart is not a possibility without an open mind.

When your partner is sitting across the room from you reading a book, you may be thinking that she's beautiful, or you may be thinking that she should talk to you instead of reading. She may glance up and see you looking at her, and say, "What are you looking at?" and you may tell yourself a story about what she means by that. If you believe what you think—"I'm getting on her nerves," "She wants to be alone," "She thinks I'm wasting time"—your reaction will have nothing to do with her. You'll just be reacting to what you think she thinks.

Meeting your thoughts with inquiry allows you to meet your partner with understanding. What determines the quality of your relationship with her is not what you think about her but whether you *believe* what you think about her. Crazy, troublemaking thoughts like "She should be paying attention to me" float into your mind uninvited: you don't even think them, they think you. Suppressing or trying to control them has never worked. But if you question those thoughts and come to understand them, they no longer have the power to disturb you or cause you to act with anything less than intelligence and kindness. You may notice that when the thoughts that once disturbed you appear, you're smiling at them as they peacefully go back to where they came from.

In this chapter you'll see people with a variety of relationship troubles do inquiry on their thoughts, using the four questions and turnaround. The passages are taken from transcripts of actual dialogues in which I asked the questions and people participating in my workshops and schools answered them. You may recognize some of the misunderstandings you've had in your own relationships and enjoy seeing how they dissolve when the thoughts behind them are questioned.

When something hurts in your relationship and it's not obvious why, you can do the same thing. Sit down and put your thoughts on paper. Concentrate on your complaints about your partner. Don't be kind. If anything, exaggerate the faults you find. Using the Worksheet on page 251 as your guide, write down how you've been wronged, what they should and shouldn't do, what you want and need from them, what you refuse to put up with any longer. And when you have it down on paper, question what you believe. Ask the four questions and turn it around.

INDEX TO DIALOGUES

Once we begin to question our thoughts, our partners, alive, dead, or divorced, are always our greatest teachers. There's no mistake about the person you're with; he or she is the perfect teacher for you, whether or not the relationship works out, and once you enter inquiry, you come to see that clearly. There's never a mistake in the universe.

So if your partner is angry, good. If there are things about him that you consider flaws, good, because these flaws are your own, you're projecting them, and you can write them down, inquire, and set yourself free. People go to India to find a guru, but you don't have to: You're living with one. Your partner will give you everything you need for your own freedom.

My Girlfriend Doesn't Make Me Happy

I resent my girlfriend, because she doesn't make me happy.

"She's supposed to make you happy"—is that true?

That's what I want.

And can you absolutely know that she's supposed to?

No.

That's a recipe for major pain. How do you react when you believe that?

Well, I get angry, and I brood, and I get very resentful.

How do you treat her when you believe that thought?

I snap at her. I speak to her disrespectfully. Sometimes I whine at her like a little kid. I don't value what she does for me. I don't appreciate her.

Who would you be without the thought that she's supposed to make you happy?

Independent and free.

And happy?

At least happier.

I would go with that. "She's supposed to make me happy"—turn it around.

I'm supposed to make me happy.

Now name three specific ways that you could make yourself happy, three things that you may not be giving yourself and that you blame her for.

Okay. I would go to more ball games with my friends. I would watch more sports on TV without feeling guilty. And I would not feel I had to have dinner with her sister and brother-in-law every time she did.

Good. You don't have to wait for anyone but you to give you those things. You can take responsibility for your own happiness and give her a break. One way you can do that is to continue to investigate your thinking and set yourself free from believing that your life is her fault. That's where true happiness is found, on the inside, and after that, you need nothing. There's another turnaround.

I'm supposed to make my girlfriend happy.

Yes, for your own sake, just because it's your own phi-losophy. Of course, you can't *make* her happy, you can't make anyone happy, that's hopeless. But you can buy her flowers, be kind to her, be generous, and take a look at yourself when you think that it's her fault that you're unhappy. You can give her what you would want in your own life. This giving can bring you hap-piness, and that's what you're seeking from her. If it comes to me to bring a cup of coffee to my husband in the morning, I make the coffee, I take it to him, and I set it down. And if he doesn't want it, I know it wasn't for him anyway. I've had a wonderful time making it, and I was only serving myself. And whether or not he wants it, when he says, "Thank you," I wonder what he's thanking me for. I bring him coffee for *my* sake, to live out my love for him. Life is a wonderful dream once we understand it.

My Wife's Demands

My wife makes too many demands on me.

Is that true? Who lives the lie and says yes when he means no? How does she make you do the things that she demands?

I feel I have to do them.

In other words, you say yes to her. You lie, you give her what you don't want to give, and you hurt yourself when you do that. And then you call it her fault. If you were honest with her, you might even say, "I *want* to want to do that for you, honey, and the truth is that I don't want to do it yet, and I may never want to. I'm working on it." Or "I don't want to do that. Can we put our heads together and find another solution?" There are so many kind and honest ways to say no. But you say yes to her because you believe you need something from her, and you do it because you're afraid that she'll withhold it from you. Egos don't love, they want something. You lie to yourself and to her when you say yes and mean no. You lie in order to get something you want her to give you. So who's more demanding, your wife or you?

I see that. I really do demand her approval.

She could make demands of you a hundred times a day, and you could say, "I love you, and no." And if she said, "If you don't do it, I'll leave you," you could say, "I understand." And then wait to see what happens. Will she leave? Will she stay? But if you tell her yes when you mean no, you've lost your integrity, you've lost yourself, and you're the one you live with. If you say yes to her and it's a lie, you lose yourself, sweetheart, and you may lose her anyway. My ex-husband could make any demands he wanted of me, and if it wasn't right for me, I would tell him the truth, I would say, for example, "I love you and I'm not able to do that." I didn't have to tell him the part that it wasn't within my integrity to do that. Often he would yell and curse and threaten to leave me, and I would say, "I understand that." And he would say, "You'll be sorry," and I would say, "You could be right, I love you, and I can't do what you're asking." But if I had told him yes when I meant no, I would have lost myself again, and I'm the one I live with. If I had said yes to him and it was a lie, I would have lost my marriage to myself. And he would have been living with a façade of a wife.

So my wife has an expectation or wish about what she should get from me, and she expresses that, and I want her to love and appreciate me, so I fulfill her expectation. If I try to stop that whole cycle, then she could leave me, and that is extremely scary.

Yes, but you've lost her anyway. You're not living with anything but an illusion. You're living with the monster in your mind, the one who will leave you if you don't do everything she wants. You haven't even met your wife yet. You're just living with your story of who she is. It's the story that scares you, not your wife.

My Husband Doesn't Care About Fixing Our Relationship

I'm angry at my husband because he doesn't care about fixing our relationship.

He's supposed to care at all about your relationship when he doesn't—does that sound like love to you? How do you treat him when you believe this insane concept that he should care about you at all, ever?

I ignore him, I judge him.

And how does it feel inside you to ignore and judge someone you love?

It hurts. I feel awful.

When you believe the thought, welcome to hell. Who would you be in his presence without the thought that he should care about you?

I would care about him.

Yes. You're trying to get love from him, and you are already love.

It always hurts to ask him for it, because it's not really coming from him then.

Yes, sweetheart. "I'm angry at my husband because he doesn't care about fixing our relationship"—turn it around.

I'm angry at myself because I don't care about fixing my relationship with me.

Hurt feelings or discomfort of any kind cannot be caused by another person. No one outside me can hurt me. That's not a possibility. It's only when I believe a stressful thought that I get hurt. And I'm the one who's hurting me by believing what I think. This is very good news, because it means that I don't have to get someone else to stop hurting me. I'm the one who can stop hurting me. It's within my power.

What we are doing with inquiry is meeting our thoughts with some simple understanding, finally. Pain, anger, and frustration will let us know when it's time to inquire. We either believe what we think or we question it: there's no other choice. Questioning our thoughts is the kinder way. Inquiry always leaves us as more loving human beings.

Yes. When you're mentally in his business, dictating whom he should or shouldn't love, you feel separation and loneliness. Can you find another turnaround?

I'm angry at myself because I don't care about fixing my relation ship with him. That's sometimes true, when I only care about making life comfortable for me.

Yes. You think, "I'll fix my relationship with him when he starts to care." And it never happens. So you may want to go home and say, "Sweetheart, I'm so excited. I love that you don't care. I just found out that I don't either."

That's true! And it's really funny!

And you may want to tell him the rest: "I found out that I don't care about you, except to make my life comfortable."

Yes.

You are everything that you call him. He is your story. So far, you haven't even met him.

My Husband Wants Too Much Sex

My husband is too sexually demanding.

Is that true? What does he demand?

Well, he doesn't exactly demand. He asks me to have sex with him.

So it's not even true that he is too sexually demanding. Interesting. And how do you react when you think he's too demanding?

I used to feel pressured and I'd try to please him by saying yes whether I felt like it or not, and now I say no most of the time.

And how do you treat him when you believe that he is demanding, and he's not? It must be a torture chamber trying to imagine what he thinks when he brings the subject up.

I'm suspicious of him. When he's nice to me, I think he's just trying to get me in the mood. It makes me tense and not at all in the mood. I see him as manipulative and sneaky, and then I think that he only cares about himself and doesn't care about my feelings. I get angry and pull away from him even more.

I can see why you're tense and turned off. Who wants to sleep with someone she believes is selfish? Who would you be without the thought that he's too demanding?

I could just give an honest yes or no when he asks me. I wouldn't imagine that he's asking me for sex all the time. If he gets grumpy when I say no, that has nothing to do with me. My only job is to ask myself if I want to have sex at that moment with that grumpy man. He might notice which man I prefer to have sex with—the grumpy one or the contented one. Right now, it feels like we'd have sex more often.

Yes. You may even see him as someone who is honestly telling you what he wants. You may see him as someone who really loves you. Look how you treat him, and he still wants to be intimate with you. "My husband is too sexually demanding"—turn it around.

I'm too sexually demanding. I often demand no sex, and I control his sex life, really. When I think my husband should be able to read my mind and ask me to have sex only when I feel like it, I'm being sexually demanding in a big way.

She Won't Give Me Unconditional Love

I am sad about my wife because she won't give me unconditional love.

"She's supposed to give you unconditional love"—is that true?

Yes.

Can you absolutely know that it's true?

Well, not absolutely, I guess.

Yes, honey. "Should" is the story of a past or future, and it's hopeless to argue with what is. How do you react when you believe that thought?

Sad, disappointed in her, sometimes angry. I withdraw from her. I feel depressed and think I deserve better. Self-pitying. Sometimes I think I married the wrong person.

Yes, because she isn't validating your dream of the ideal wife. Who would you be if you didn't believe the thought that she's supposed to give you unconditional love? Who would you be in her presence if you never believed that thought again?

I'd be someone who didn't expect unconditional love from her.

What I'm hearing is that *you* would love *her* unconditionally, however conditionally she loved you. As long as you believe she should give you unconditional love, you're not talking about the wife you live with. You're talking about the wife in your imagination, and not giving your unconditional love to the wife you live with. So let's turn it around.

I am sad because I won't give her unconditional love. But I really do love her. I believe that you should love your partner unconditionally—that's what I committed to when we married, and it's what I do.

Look a little deeper, sweetheart. See if you can find three genuine ways that you don't give her unconditional love. You don't sound very loving when you get angry at her and withdraw.

Well, that's true. I wasn't feeling very loving then. Okay, I guess it's true that I don't love her unconditionally when I think she doesn't love me unconditionally. I get resentful, and I close my heart. That's true.

Is there another way you don't love her unconditionally?

We have arguments about money. The other day I got angry at her when she said we couldn't afford to buy the new boat I wanted. She was right, actually, and I acted as though it wasn't true and was cold and nasty to her. That really hurts now.

Well, sweetheart, when you go home this evening admit that she was right. Apologize from your heart, the way you're feeling now. Ask her how you can make it right—and really listen to what she has to say, without defending a position. She'll take you where you really want to go, if you're serious about this unconditional love that you want in your life. Humility is the opposite of subservience and the beginning of you stepping into your power, angel. Can you find one more example?

Yes. I punish her for not being as attractive as other women, for gaining so much weight. The crazy thing is that I don't really even care. I love her so much—she looks beautiful to me. I criticize what she eats—and I'm the one who could take a look at that in my own life. And I see that that's the other turnaround: "I should love myself unconditionally." And I often don't.

Can you find three genuine ways that you don't love yourself unconditionally?

When I eat too much, I see myself in a very cruel way. I use self-hatred as an appetite controller—not that it works. Also, I'm sometimes disgusted with myself when I think I have made a mistake. And I really give myself a hard time when I forget things.

Yes, honey. Feel the violence that you inflict on yourself. And look at the pain you cause yourself when you compare your wife with someone who doesn't exist, the ideal wife, someone who *can't* exist—in any marriage. That's not giving yourself love. And you already know it's not giving her love. And sweetheart, it's only in the moment, it's not forever. We don't love conditionally or unconditionally forever. It keeps changing: "I love you," "I don't," "I do," "I do," "I don't." And when you don't, it's always going to be you in the way, not your wife, you can count on that, so sit down and inquire and get real with your answers and your sweet innocent self. It can't ever be something outside you, a situation or a person, that is causing your unhappiness. It can only be your unquestioned thinking about that situation or person. There's no exception to that.

I Need Him to Understand Me

I need my husband to understand me.

"You need him to understand you"—is that true?

Yes.

Is that what you really need? Can you absolutely know that that's what is best for you?

Well, ultimately . . . I guess not.

Who knows what's best for you right now? Does a flower open ahead of its time? It isn't possible, is it? We can give it care, sunshine, water, and it opens when it opens: right on time. Sweetheart, how do you treat him when you believe the thought that you need him to understand you, and he doesn't?

I get really angry and upset. I withdraw. I stand in judgment of him.

Yes, when you believe that, you don't understand *him!* So you are the teacher of no understanding. Who would you be without the thought that you need him to understand you?

I would be happy with him.

Yes, honey. You'd understand him. You'd be the living example of understanding, which is what you want him to be. When I seek someone's love, approval, or appreciation, how can I possibly understand him? It's unkind to him, and it's unkind to myself. I would rather be free. I would rather see what happens in that freedom, just being with him and accepting him as he is in the moment. Who knows what I could learn? And who wouldn't love and appreciate someone who understands? "I need him to understand me"—turn it around.

I need me to understand him.

Yes. You need to understand that he doesn't understand. You just gave him his life back, in your mind, and he will experience that, and as he does, it comes back to you again in the sweet space that flows without separation. When you believe the thought "My husband should understand me," and the reality is that he doesn't, it's a recipe for unhappiness. You can do everything in the world to make him understand you, and he'll end by understanding what he understands.

My Girlfriend Shouldn't Leave Me

I am saddened that she might leave me.

"She shouldn't leave you"—can you absolutely know that that's true? Can you absolutely know that that wouldn't be for your highest good if she left you, that you wouldn't have a better life without her?

No, I can't know that. It's very hard to imagine, though.

And how do you react when you believe the thought "She shouldn't leave me" when she wants to leave?

Insecure. Miserable.

A feeling of being left? How do you react when you believe that she might leave you? How do you treat her when you feel insecure and miserable?

It only takes one clear person to
have a good relationship.

I'm clingy and I sulk. I watch her all the time. I do exactly the things that would make her leave me.

Yes. Are you starting to see your innocence? We would all change if we knew how. And you don't know how, so the ego just gets a bigger plan. And that doesn't work either. It's all a scam you run on yourself. Only integrity works. And how have you lived with her when you were trying to be "the one"? Do you smile when you don't feel like it? Do you say yes when you mean no?

I give when I don't feel I have anything to give.

Yes, that's how you react when you believe this thought. You don't have a life, you lose yourself to the effort of gaining her approval. People aren't attached to people, they're attached to their beliefs. Who would you be without the thought that she shouldn't leave you?

I'd be much calmer. I wouldn't be worrying so much.

"I am saddened that she might leave me"—turn it around.

I am saddened that I might leave myself.

When you mentally go out of your business into hers, when you mentally go into "She will leave me," you've left yourself. Whose business is it whom you live with?

Mine.

And whose business is it whom she lives with?

It's hers.

Yes, honey. Believing the thought that your partner shouldn't leave you is like saying, "I want you to be with me even if that's not what you want. I don't really care what's best for you. And by the way, I love you." That doesn't feel like love to me. Without the belief that your partner should want to stay with you, you can join her totally in her plans for leaving you.

That sounds very difficult.

Is that true? Who would you be without the thought that she should stay? See if you can really go there.

It would actually be a relief not to be locked onto the idea that she should stay. There would be more breathing space in my life. I'd be open to possibilities.

And who would you be, looking at her without the thought "She should stay"?

I can see that I'd be really happy if she were happy. She should go if that's what she wants. I'd be fine.

Yes, sweetheart. Can you find another turnaround?

I am saddened that I might leave her. I do leave her emotionally when I think she shouldn't leave me.

You leave her when you think she shouldn't have a life except for the life you think she should have. You leave who she really is, and instead you live with a terrifying woman who might leave you at any moment. There's another turnaround—can you find it?

Hmm . . . I am happy *that she might leave me? Even that could be true.*

Because then you get to discover yourself. You get to focus not on her but on you and your own thinking, which is the cause of all your suffering.

Up to now the idea of being alone has always been connected with sadness and panic.

When we investigate our thinking and come to realize what is true, we're never lonely again, whether we have a partner or not.

I'm Unlovable

Other people are cute and generous, or funny, or brave and strong. I'm not. I am unlovable, and that makes me desperately unhappy.

Sweetheart, do you want to know the truth?

Yes.

"You're unlovable"—is that true?

It's what I think. No one ever really loved me, not even my mother. She never hugged me when I was little, and she was always shouting at me and rushing out the door to get to her job.

Your mother was always rushing out the door to get to her job, and that means she doesn't love you? Is that true?

She may have been too tired to hug us and talk to us much, I can see that. She did have to support me and my brother on her own.

Wasn't that love?

Could be.

"I am unlovable"—can you absolutely know that that's true?

No, I can't know that. But I still feel it.

Of course you feel it, because you believe that thought. That's why we're questioning the thought. Pain seems to be a great motivator at the beginning. Later on, you may find that you don't need it. How do you react when you believe a thought that you don't even know is true?

Heavy. I lose all spontaneity. I'm lonely, and I long for what I can't have. Nothing else seems to matter, so I don't do much except stay home and try to escape from the thought by watching television and eating when I'm not even hungry.

Who would you be without the thought "I'm unlovable"?

Oh, I'd be very much lighter. I can see myself walking down the street just liking the falling leaves and the sunlight. I would feel much closer to the people I know and I'd be interested in them— instead of in why they don't love me. I might take a vacation by myself and enjoy it, or maybe I'd ask someone to come. That could be fun too.

Turn it around.

People are unlovable. Yes, when I believe that I'm unlovable, I am so full of sadness and resentments I can't love anyone else.

Can you find another turnaround?

I'm lovable.

Can you see how that is more honest?

It's hard to see. I really want to, but it's hard.

Find three genuine ways that you're lovable.

Hmm. That's really hard. . . . Okay, here's one. I have a nice smile.

Good, sweetheart. That's a very good find.

And I've been a good sister. I've always been there for my brother.

That's two. Can you find one more?

Hmm. Nothing else comes to me.

Find one thing that you did today that you find lovable.

Well, I fed the squirrels.

Yes. That was kind of you. That's three. The fact is that you are lovable, whether you like it or not. There's nothing you can do about it.

She Shouldn't Be in So Much Pain

She shouldn't be in so much pain.

Is that true?

Yes. I hate to see her that way.

Can you absolutely know that that's true? Who needs God when we have *your* opinion?

I guess I can't really know that.

No, you can't, sweetheart. This understanding could be the beginning of your freedom. Her pain is *her* business. How do you react when you believe that she shouldn't be in so much pain, and there's nothing you can do about it?

It hurts a lot.

Yes, it adds your pain onto hers, and now we have two people in pain. And it doesn't help her at all. Who would you be without this belief?

Free to just be there for her.

Yes, and it would be easier for you to be with her. You would be more available if you weren't in pain over her pain. You would be more able to be completely present with her.

My Parents Should Love and Appreciate Me

Parents should love and appreciate their sons.

"Parents should love and appreciate their sons"—is that true?

Yes, it fucking is true!

That's a good one. Can you absolutely know that that's true?

Yes!

Oh, so we're supposed to stop our lives and love and appreciate you? I don't think so! That is an insane thought, because it argues with reality. How do I know that parents shouldn't love and appreciate their children? They don't—sometimes. No wonder you're so angry. How do you react when you believe the thought that we as parents should love and appreciate and validate you, and we don't?

A lifetime of pain.

Yes, it's a very painful thought. That thought is a childhood toy of torture that you can put aside now. The truth will set you free, if you're up for it. Who would you be if you never had that thought again—if you were incapable of thinking it, if, no matter how hard you tried, it just wouldn't come back?

I'd be free and at peace.

So, "Parents should love and appreciate their sons"— can you absolutely know that it's true? Go inside and listen to the answer.

There's a very strong voice inside me that says it should be that way.

Of course there is. You've been feeding it like Cookie Monster! And you've been passing it on to your wife and children and any of us who hang out with you, getting us to agree that it's true. You want us to appreciate you and see what a victim you are, and eventually we get tired of it, so it validates what you believe about parents, all the way through the whole world, your whole life! So go inside, sweetheart, because only your own truth will set you free, not ours. There's no right or wrong answer. And until you come to your truth, you'll just keep believing what you think. It's awful to be happy and free all the time: How are you going to connect with us and manipulate us and be a victim if you're happy? You think you'd lose your whole life if you gave up that belief. You wouldn't even know how to live. "Parents should love and appreciate their sons"—can you absolutely know that that's true? *Did* they love and appreciate you? Not according to you. So how do you know that they shouldn't have loved and appreciated you? Because they didn't. That's reality!

Oh. Can it be that simple?

I think you just got the answer. "Parents should love and appreciate their sons"—turn it around.

I should love and appreciate myself.

That's it! There's no one else, sweetheart, because according to you, your parents didn't. You're the only one left.

I Should Be His One and Only

I'm angry with my husband because he didn't dump his other women and choose me as his one and only.

"Your life would be much better if he dumped them"—is that true?

Well, it's pretty obvious to me that it would be better.

And can you absolutely know that it would be better?

No.

How do you react when you believe the thought that he should dump the other women?

I try to undermine them. I try to convince him to be monogamous. I'm always jealous. I think of them constantly and of him with them. I constantly compare myself with them. Am I prettier than this one? Am I smarter than that one?

For the personality, love is nothing more than agreement. If I agree with you, you love me. And the minute I don't agree with you, the minute I question one of your sacred beliefs, I become your enemy; you divorce me in your mind. Then you start looking for all the reasons why you're right, and you stay focused outside yourself. When you're focused outside and believe that your problem is caused by someone else, rather than by your attachment to the story you're believing in the moment, then you are your own victim, and the situation appears to be hopeless.

That's a very painful way to live, sweetheart. It's painful
to try to manipulate the man you love, to spend your
time plotting how you can get rid of people he loves
or wondering if you're as good as they are. Whose
business is it whom he sleeps with?

I hate this question.

You hate it because you're holding on to your pain for
dear life. You're holding on to your thoughts of "I'm
right and he's wrong. I'm the good one and he's the vil-
lain." Would you rather be right or free?

I'd rather be free. I really would. I've had enough of this misery.

So whose business is it whom he sleeps with?

It's his business. I know that. It's his business, not mine.

And whose business is it whom you sleep with?

It's my business.

"He should sleep with you only"—is that true? What's
the reality of it? He doesn't. He sleeps with other
women. That's the reality of it. It doesn't go along with
our morality, it doesn't go along with what society
would teach us, it's what is. It's an outright lie that he
should sleep with you only, when he doesn't. What
happens inside you when you believe the thought that
he shouldn't sleep with other women?

I hate him.

And how does that feel inside you?

Awful. I just want to die.

And how do you treat him when you believe the thought that he should be faithful to you?

I rage at him. I cut myself off. I close my heart.

Is that pretty painful?

It's horrible.

The reason you experience pain and loneliness is that you're mentally in his business, and it doesn't leave anyone here present with you. Of *course* you're lonely! She's over there with him, you're over there with him, everyone's over there with him, and there's no one here with you. You think he's supposed to be with you, but *you* can't even do it. He leaves you, you leave you—what's the difference? The way to stay present is to question your thoughts. "He shouldn't sleep with other women"—is that true? "I would be much better off if he were with me and not her"—can you absolutely know that that's true? He's not responsible for your misery, you are. You're believing a lie, and that's what is causing your pain. Can you see a reason to drop this thought that argues with reality, "He should sleep with me only"?

Yes. I hate to suffer.

I see we come from the same school. And please don't try to drop it. No one can drop a thought. We're just seeing a reason to drop it. Can you see a reason to believe that thought that doesn't hurt?

No.

Who would you be without that thought?

I wouldn't hate him so much. Maybe I wouldn't feel so betrayed. I don't know if I could ever open my heart to him again, but at least I would be more understanding.

Sweetheart, an open mind is an open heart. Who knows what you would feel or how you would treat him if you didn't believe your thoughts about him? Who would you be, in his presence, if you didn't believe the thought that he should get rid of his other women? Close your eyes, picture him with them, look at his face without any belief that he should choose you. Can you see him?

Yes. He's beautiful. He looks happy.

That's unconditional love. That's who you really are. Now turn it around.

I'm angry with me because I didn't choose me as my one and only. I carried all those other women around in my head with me.

Turn it around again.

I'm angry with me because I chose him as my one and only. That makes sense to me.

Yes, if you want to be monogamous, you can say, "Sweetheart, I love you just the way you are, I love it that you want ten women, I want you to have what you want, and I need to leave you now. I'm monogamous, and I want a monogamous partner." That's choosing him as your one and only, the one you love, unchanged; it's just that you don't live with him now. But whether you stay with him or leave him, you never have to close your heart. And then you may notice that the next person in front of you is your one and only, in the moment when he's with you, and that you don't require him to be anything but what he is. Unconditional love doesn't need to dictate the form.

My Lover Should Give Me Sex

I want her to give me sex. I feel unloved when she doesn't.

What do you want from sex?

Orgasm and connection.

Let's look at these one at a time. "You want her to give you orgasms"—is that true?

Yes.

An orgasm is what you're getting your ecstasy from, and you're making her responsible for your ecstasy, so that you don't have to be responsible. "You want her to give you orgasms"—is that really true?

Maybe not, when I look at it that way.

It's good to get real. To want an orgasm keeps you from it. When you're supposed to have it, it will be there. If an orgasm is really what you wanted, you'd be masturbating, and I know that that's not the same for you. It's your mind that wants the orgasm and wants her to play her role in it. Without the thought, where's the want, where's the need? There's just you, perfectly satisfied. And that could look like sex or not. What was the other thing you wanted sex for?

Connection. I want a connection with her.

You can't *not* connect with her! You think that because there are two separate bodies, as it appears, there are two separate minds. Without the stressful thoughts that separate us from one another, there is only one mind, and it's everywhere. Bodies can't be connected; you can only connect with your own mind, and it encompasses her and all of us. Connection can only be made from inside you. You can't connect with her. There's no point in trying, because you're already connected. You can only connect with yourself and come to see how that connects you with her. Now turn your statement around.

I want me to give me orgasms.

That's all that ever happens.

I want a connection with myself.

It always comes down to you with you. As long as you look at sex as the thing you're missing, if she doesn't give you sex you sever your connection. One reason we like sex is that when we're really into it, we are "out of our minds": we enter the space between thoughts. But if we're using sex for that because we don't know another way to escape from our painful thoughts or connect with our partner, eventually the thoughts are there even during sex, and soon we're looking at the clock: When will he be finished? And even wonderful sex may no longer be so wonderful. Eventually, every Band-Aid stops working, and our painful thoughts ooze out. Only the truth can set us free, only the truth can stop the pain, and only with the truth can we be truly intimate. The next time it hurts when she doesn't give you sex, question your thoughts. Maybe instead of sex you'll find love.

I Am Nothing Without My Boyfriend

I am nothing without my boyfriend.

How do you react when you believe the thought that you don't have a life without him, that there is no you without him?

I feel like I'd do anything and everything to have him.

No, not to have him—that's not possible, how can you "have" someone? He is not the problem; having him or not having him is never the problem. You believe that without him there is no you, and you do everything in your power to make that belief real. You are fighting for your life, and you call it fighting for him. That's why people get guns and shoot their lovers. "If I can't have a life, then he's not going to have a life either, and neither is she." They believe that murder is justified, because without their lover they think they have no life. "He has taken my life, so it's only fair for me to take his." That's the thinking that creates a hell. "I'm nothing without him"—who would you be if you didn't believe that? It's pretty scary, because it means you've been wrong for your whole life. Welcome to heaven. This is where it begins, in humility. "I am wrong. I've been confused." "Without him you have no life"—is that true?

No, I've just been too scared to find out.

You use him so that you don't have to look at your own fear. "I'll just focus on him and capture him, and do whatever it takes, there's no price too high." Turn it around: "*With* him I have no life, I am nothing." That's just how you've been living. If you think you're nothing without him, you have to think you're nothing even with him. You're a woman pretending to be his total servant and hating it.

And imposing on his life.

Only always. It's not love.

I don't want to do that to him.

Yes, sweetheart. And also turn it around.

I don't want to do that to me.

Yes. When you do that to you, you do that to him, and then you get it back again, because what you do to him you do to yourself. If you don't like yourself, why would he? If you don't want to be with yourself, how can you expect him to want to be with you? If you think you're nothing, that's what you bring to us, and we mirror back to you that you're nothing. It's all your story.

Only you can kick yourself out of paradise. So if you are Adam and you look to Eve for completion, you have just kicked yourself out of paradise. You could just experience your own nature, which is to love yourself, and therefore her, with no separation. But if you want something from her, if you think you need her love or approval, you suffer. There's only one way I can use you to complete me, and that is if I judge you, inquire, and turn it around.

My Father Shouldn't Be So Passive

I don't like my father being so passive when mother asks him what he wants her to make him for supper. He says things like "Anything you make is fine" or "I don't know; you decide." I just hate that.

He sounds like a saint.

Who sounds like a saint?

Your father. He leaves it to her. That sounds sweet and generous.

But my mother is so disappointed that he doesn't state his preference.

Because she thinks he should have preferences. He's probably telling her the truth. If I were your mother, I would believe him and cook my favorite meals every day. If he didn't love that, he would say so, and I would find out, and in the meantime I would love it when mealtimes rolled around, and I would adore the person I was living with. Look at the options that he gives her. It could be that because she has preferences, she thinks that he should have them too. And you think that he should make something up. Do you say to yourself, "I could make something up to please her"?

Well, I do make something up, and it does please her.

Good, honey, if your choices were true for you. And did you sell out? Your father didn't. He really didn't have preferences. I would believe him.

Wow. I can see that. I sold out, and he didn't. I gave her what she wanted.

That's very sweet. And was it within your integrity? Was it honest for you to do that?

I did it to please her. I would do anything to please her.

I hear you, sweetheart. And what did you want from her? It could have been within your integrity—that's why I'm asking. What was it? Let's take this direction, honey: Can you know that the answers he gave your mother were not decisive answers for him? "It's up to you. I don't have a preference." That sounds pretty decisive.

It does when you put it that way. Hmm.

"Your father should have given her what she wanted"— is that true? Can you know that that's for his highest good, or hers?

Well, it wouldn't have taken much time to make something up and get her off his back.

Interesting. "They would both be better off if he would just come up with something to appease her"—can you absolutely know that that's true?

I would have been better off if it hadn't fallen to me to do that.

And how do you react when you believe the thought that he should change for your sake? Did you get to be right? Were you the good one of the two of you? Were you the example of what your father should be? What else did you get?

I got his jealousy and rage.

What else did you get for appeasing her, and being right, and doing what you thought his job was if he had been a good husband? Was it ever enough?

Thinking that people are supposed to do or be anything other than what they are is like saying that the tree over there should be the sky. I investigated that and found freedom.

No, but I got a continuing relationship with her. My father didn't leave.

We could say that the family stayed together, but it doesn't always feel that way inside us. It feels pretty separated sometimes.

My father is jealous, angry, and abusive to me.

Turn it around.

I am jealous, angry, and abusive to my father.

Yes? And how does it feel to live that way, especially in your mind?

Pretty lousy.

"He should give in to her the way I do. He should sacrifice his happiness for hers the way I do." That's confusion, honey, and confusion is the only suffering in this universe. When you question your thoughts and get a little clarity going, you can begin to see him and appreciate him for who he really is. He did none of the things that you did, and she's still with him, she didn't leave him. It could be that they have a very sweet thing going that you just don't understand. Who knows?

I Want Tons of Approval

I want tons of approval.

Is that true? Is that what you really want?

Approval would be very nice.

Hopeless! We're too busy to approve of you: we're too busy trying to get *your* approval. And once you have our approval, what are you going to do with it?

I don't know.

How does it feel when you constantly seek our approval? Isn't that your main career, seeking approval?

Yes. It's not very comfortable.

And how do you treat us when you want our approval and we don't give it? You have a huge investment in us, you've sacrificed your life for our approval, and when we don't give it, how do you treat us?

Not very nicely.

"We should give you our approval"—turn it around.

I should give me my approval.

Yes, because you're the only one left! If we want something from you and you give it to us, then we approve, and if you don't give it to us, we don't approve. It's simple. We're just like you. Sweetheart, let's look at that turnaround, "I should give me my approval." Now give me three things about you that you approve of. It could be anything, as long as it's genuine.

Okay, let's see. When I lend money to people, I understand if they can't pay me back right away or at all; I don't hold grudges. Two, I show up on time; I don't like to be late. One more, huh? I'm a good friend.

Good, honey. The original statement doesn't seem to work as well for you. Can you find another turnaround?

"If you don't seek our approval, there's no way you can ever have it"—can you really know that that's true? You just act sometimes as if you're God, as if you need to make things happen. I noticed that things happen with or without me, people approve of me or they don't. It has nothing to do with me. This is really good news, since it leaves me responsible for my own happiness. It leaves me to do nothing but live my life as kindly and intelligently as I can. If you don't notice and aren't grateful, I understand. It's only me I'm dealing with, and that is enough for a lifetime.

I don't need their approval.

I can tell you that when I have people's approval is when I need it. How do I know that I need their approval? I have it. How do I know that I don't need their approval? I don't have it. And in either case, it has nothing to do with me. It's their story about me that they're approving of. What's important is: Am I living in ways that I myself approve of? When I question my thoughts, I like the mind I live with. It not only leaves me alone, it leaves you alone too. That's very peaceful, and I love it.

I don't need their approval.

My Father Treated Me Badly

I'm saddened that my father treated me badly and put me down all the time. He should have loved and appreciated me. I want him to love me and tell me about himself and his pain, and I never want to experience being denied love and approval again.

"He put you down all the time"—is that true?

Yes. And it really hurt.

Is it true that he put you down *all* the time? Every single moment?

Well, not every single moment.

Can you find a time when he didn't put you down?

You mean when he was eating breakfast or reading his paper?

Yes, that's a beginning. Can you find a moment when he was nice to you?

Almost never.

Can you find a single moment?

Well, he took me to the zoo once. That was fun.

So "He put you down all the time"—is that true?

Almost all the time. Most of the time, I'd say.

Just answer with a simple yes or a simple no. Nothing else satisfies the mind. It has to know what's real or it lives its life trying to prove what it thinks, and it can never rest. "He put you down all the time"—is that true?

No.

And how do you react when you believe that he put you down all the time?

Sad and resentful. Deprived of a happy childhood. Sometimes I'm furious at him.

Who would you be without that thought?

A little lighter. Less resentful. Maybe I'd be able to remember other times like the day at the zoo.

"He put you down all the time"—turn it around.

He didn't put me down all the time.

Isn't that truer?

Yes.

We're like children, honey, we believe our thoughts literally. Can you find another turnaround?

I put me down all the time. That's true. I've been very hard on myself.

Yes, sweetheart. We've been a little confused. "Fathers are supposed to appreciate their daughters"—is that true? On what planet? Some fathers are too out of their minds with the fear of a nonexistent future to even notice that they have a daughter in front of them. They're so anxious about their sweet daughter's welfare that they miss the daughter.

Well, I really think he should have appreciated me.

And what's the reality of it? Did he?

No.

Then that's what's true, sweetheart, in your opinion. He didn't, sometimes. Can you absolutely know that he should have appreciated you? Can you know that ultimately that was the best thing for you?

No, I can't know that.

So, "He should have appreciated me"—how do you react to that thought?

It feels like I don't even get my feet off the ground, that's how bad I feel sometimes.

Who would you be without the thought?

I think I'd feel a lot better. Lighter, I'd say. I wouldn't feel so heavy and so disappointed.

"He should have appreciated me"—turn it around.

I should have appreciated me. That's certainly true.

Can you find another turnaround?

I should have appreciated him. But how could I? I was just a little girl who wanted his love.

We're just looking at possibilities, sweetheart. Little girls don't have inquiry. Can you find another turnaround?

Hmm.

"He shouldn't . . ."

He shouldn't have appreciated me?

So, honey, give me three ways that your life is better because he didn't appreciate you.

Three ways? Let's see. Well, one way is that I've become very independent. I like that about myself. And two, I've learned to be really conscious of other people and to appreciate them in my life. Though I haven't done that with my father, yet. And three, I spent more time with my mother. We're very close as a result.

What did your father say to you to put you down?

Oh, things like "You're in my way." "You're not doing it well enough." Like that, all the time. Oops—a lot of the time.

And did you ever experience the same thing?

What do you mean?

Turn it around, see how it sounds. "He's in my way"— does that sound true?

Yes, when the thought of him stops me from getting on with my life.

Are there any other ways to turn it around that might be truer?

I'm in my way when I think that he's in my way. I'm in my way by still seeking his love. That's so true.

What about "You're not doing it well enough"? How would you turn that around?

He's not doing it well enough. He's not being a good enough father.

For you, honey. I would question that later.

I see that I'm judging him.

Let's look at your next statement.

I want my father to love me and talk to me about himself.

Turn it around.

I want myself to love me and talk to me about myself.

It's not his job, and it doesn't appear to be his interest, in your opinion.

Actually, he's been dead for a while.

Is that true? He seems to be very much alive here today. Let's go back to the time when you were a little girl, okay? He should stop and tell you about himself. Did you ask him?

No.

"Fathers should be psychic"—is that true? Sweetheart, I hear from you that he had no way of knowing that you even wanted to know about him or that you were interested in his life. Little girls don't know how to ask.

Right.

We work with it now, and your life can be radically different as a result. So this Work is very precious. Since that little girl wanted her father to tell her about his life, she is the teacher who has taught you to just ask: "Tell me about your life." We begin now. How does it feel when you believe the thought "He should tell me about his life," and you don't ask, and he doesn't tell you? Let's look at that one.

I've been judging him and making him really wrong.

So how did you live when you believed that thought?

Well, I basically cut him out of my life. There was really no way he could come to me anymore, because I had it set in my mind that he wouldn't.

And how did it feel to be fatherless in the years before he died?

Isolated. Cold.

That describes how many people view death. Can you see a reason to drop this thought, "I want him to tell me about his life"?

Yes. Because it just causes pain, nothing but pain.

Who would you be without this thought?

I'd be fresh and right there, moment by moment, and trying it again and again, just asking for what I want.

"I want him to tell me about his life"—turn it around.

I want to tell myself about my life.

That's just what you're doing now. We're looking at your internal life and your life growing up with your father, and how you abandoned him. He didn't abandon you. It was the other way around. You didn't ask.

Yes.

You can begin now. Let's look at the next statement.

My father shouldn't treat me badly. He should talk to me about his pain.

Is that true?

No. Not from where I'm sitting now. I see that he should have treated me as he did, because he did—it was all he could do. And he shouldn't have told me about his pain if he didn't.

Turn it around.

I shouldn't treat him badly. I should talk to myself about his pain. Yes. That's hard to hear, but it's really true. I see how I treated him. No wonder he didn't feel close to me. I shut him out when he didn't agree with me or give me what I wanted. I just got a glimpse of the hurt look on his face. I was only about ten years old. I was so cold, all-knowing. No wonder he didn't want to talk to me about his pain.

Can you find another turnaround?

I shouldn't treat myself badly. I should talk to myself about my pain.

Is that as true or truer?

Yes. I can see how I hurt myself by costing me my father. I even see other men the way I believed that he was. I feel so bad about this. How long does it last?

Not long, honey. You're just sorting things out now. Be gentle with yourself, and continue.

But I was so totally selfish!

You were a little girl, believing what she believed. We live our lives out of what we believe. Thoughts can be very painful until they're questioned, and you're doing that now.

Yeah.

That's what this is about: just taking a look to see what was your part in it. That's where the pain is created, discovered, and uncreated.

Yes.

Let's look at the next one.

I need my father to love me.

"Your father didn't love you"—is that true? Was it ever true in your whole life?

No. I can see that now. I was okay, more than okay. He loved me.

How do you react when you believe the thought "My father doesn't love me"? How did you react when you were a little girl?

I made myself totally small and didn't recognize that I had all this love in me. And I wasn't able to see his love for me. It's amazing. I'm seeing it today as if for the first time.

Who would you be, growing up, without the thought
"My father doesn't love me"?

*It would be just me. I would be free, really. It would be so much
easier to love him.*

Maybe you wouldn't be getting in his way with the
motivation of manipulating his love. Let's turn it around.

I don't love myself. Yes, that is much truer.

Can you find another turnaround?

*My father does love me. Yes, I can see that now. It makes me want
to cry, in a good way.*

Sweetheart, this is something you can do at home. Sit
with your eyes closed and watch him and the ways
that he loved you, from your earliest memory all the
way up to the last time you saw him. Allow as many
memories as you can to surface. Just watch him without your story and with an open mind. Do this for a
few days, and as you watch him, write down any troubling beliefs and get your father back into your heart.
If you're experiencing any kind of pain, confusion, or
discomfort around him, just investigate your thinking.
Ask four questions, turn it around, and have a happy
life. When you're thorough about this, the thought
of him becomes a sweet visit every time. You begin
to realize that you love your father with all of your
heart and just couldn't express it as a child. We're all
children when we believe what we think about our
fathers. Your father didn't love you the way that you
wanted him to, and that doesn't mean that he didn't
love you. How *you* can love you, how *you* can father

you—that's what you're learning now. It's always a beginning.

My Ex-wife Should Forgive Me

I am sad that after ten years of separation she's still not willing to forgive me.

Whose business is it if you forgive?

Mine.

Whose business is her forgiveness?

Not mine.

I love that you noticed, sweetheart. It's her business whom she forgives. Turn it around.

After ten years of separation I am still not willing to forgive myself.

Isn't that as true?

Yes.

There's another turnaround. Can you find it?

After ten years of separation I am still not willing to forgive her.

Tell me about that.

I don't know where to start.

So she is supposed to forgive you? When you know how to start, *you* forgive *her,* and then go talk to her about forgiveness. Look how you live when you want understanding. It's very painful. Understanding is *your* job. You're the one who should understand you. Let's look at your next statement.

I want her to be open and willing to talk.

Whose business is her openness, or whom she wants to talk to?

It's hers.

Can you see how, after ten years, you still want to control her thinking, her timing, her sadness, her very existence? You want to control how open she is. You want to control whom she talks to. You even want to control her forgiveness. It's hopeless. Who would you be without this thought? Honest, living truthfully, not crawling on your belly for forgiveness or love, just an honest, loving man, a man who respects where she is at, wherever that may be. Let's look at the next one.

I want her to leave me in peace.

Whose business is it whom she leaves alone? When you said yes to her requests, what did you want in exchange, what were you buying? You wanted her to forgive you, to say nice things to your son about you. And were you honest with her about it? Did you say, "Here's the deal: I'll give you money if you say nice things to our son about me. I'll give you money and in return you'll pretend to forgive me"?

No.

So the next time you talk to her, you may want to tell her that. This is integrity. If she says, "No, I won't do that," you can thank her for her integrity, and let her know that she is your teacher, and how wonderful it is that she couldn't be bribed. And eventually you may notice that forgiveness is automatic; it comes as soon as you understand your own stressful thoughts. You see that your pain is never her fault, ever. And if *she* can't see that, she can't truly forgive you. It has nothing to do with you.

I'll Lose My Girlfriend if I Tell the Truth

I told my girlfriend that I'm interested in someone else, and she threatened to leave me. Now I think my honesty could end my relationship and leave me lonely. I'm afraid I'll lose her by telling the truth.

If you're afraid that you'll lose her or that you won't get what you want, then you definitely have a problem. How do you react when you believe the thought that you'll lose her if you tell the truth?

Scared. I don't tell her what I really think or want to tell her. I lie to her, which makes me feel awful. I feel separate and lonely. I tell myself I'm a failure. I withdraw and beat myself up for not being able to do this right.

Who would you be without the belief that you'll lose her if you tell the truth?

Comfortable, and maybe more honest with myself. Maybe more honest with my girlfriend.

Being honest is very easy when you're not afraid of losing something. It's the simplest thing—and more satisfying than anything you might think you could get from outside you. You become a lover of what is. You no longer seek the perfect relationship. Instead of seeking, you find—always. What we want is right in front of our noses. So, turn it around.

I'll lose her if I lie. I'll lose myself if I lie. That is truer for me. I hurt myself and her more with the lying. I won't lose something if I tell the truth. I have experienced not losing after being honest; in fact, I've noticed that I usually gain more.

That's my experience 100 percent. Let's look at your next statement.

I want sharing the truth to not hurt, disappoint, or anger people. Sometimes I'm not honest because I think it isn't kind.

"You can hurt or disappoint people with your truth"— is that true?

It seems that way.

If I really believe that telling my truth would hurt someone's feelings, I don't tell it. I stop. I don't go past my own idea of what could hurt you because that would hurt me. These are my own boundaries. I can't know that it would hurt your feelings. I stop for the sake of my own feelings. I don't walk around being careful about what I say; I stop for myself. I am responsible for my own heaven or hell. On the other hand, if you ask me point-blank for the truth, then I'm going to tell you. I want to give you everything I see, if you ask. The way you hear my answer is what determines whether it hurts you or helps you. So every person is responsible for himself, in the giving and receiving. I could say the most loving thing, and someone's feelings could be hurt. The story they tell about what they *think* I said is how they hurt their own feelings. Nothing else is possible. If I ask you a question point-blank and you dance around it, thinking that your truth will hurt me, then you're not honoring yourself or me. To not answer honestly could leave you feeling incomplete. Since I asked you straight up, it must mean I can handle it. Can you really know that you can hurt or disappoint another person with your words?

No. I can't know that.

How do you react when you believe that thought?

I become very conflicted. It feels like an impossible situation.

Who would you be without it?

Relaxed. Free to be honest. Free to be me. Living in my integrity.

Turn it around.

I want sharing the truth to not hurt, disappoint, or anger me. That's good.

Let's look at your next statement.

Honesty is scary and frightening sometimes.

Turn it around.

Honesty is not scary or frightening. I can see that. It's not the honesty I'm scared of. It's the loss.

Yes, honey. It's good that you see that the loss is the gain, always. What was the next thought?

How do we love ourselves? One way is by not seeking approval outside ourselves—that's my experience. By not seeking approval outside myself, I come to see that I already have it. I don't want approval; I want people to think the way they think. If I seek your approval, it's not comfortable. And I've come to see, through inquiry, that what you approve of is what I want. That's love—it wouldn't change anything.

Honesty opposes getting what I want. That's not true. Lying opposes getting what I want.

That's what I love about what we really want—it's such a surprise. To be honest is to live closer to your true nature. The way I know that it is, is that when you're not living it, it hurts. That hurt is an opportunity to notice what stressful thought you're believing in the moment, to question it and turn it around. That's what all pain is about. Sanity doesn't suffer—ever.

My Husband Should Come Back to the Family

My husband should come back to the family.

Can you absolutely know that that's true?

I desperately want it.

And can you absolutely know that it's true that he should come back?

No, I can't.

Inquiry only deals with reality. The reality is that he hasn't come back. He shouldn't come back until he does. When you believe the thought that he should come back, you're arguing with reality, and when you do that, you lose, but only 100 percent of the time. It's like trying to teach a cat to bark. You're saying, "I'm going to devote my whole life to teaching that cat to bark." And you teach it and teach it, and at the end of ten years, the cat looks up at you and says, "Meow." There is something that will make you much happier than your husband coming back, and your belief keeps you from being aware of it. Can you find what that is? How do you react when you believe the thought "My husband should come back to the family"?

I am miserable, angry, depressed, bitter.

And how do you talk to him, how do you talk about him to your children, when you believe your husband should come back, and he doesn't come back, and you're miserable and bitter like this?

I'm not very nice.

Be specific. Close your eyes. What pictures of yourself do you see?

I see myself criticizing him, shouting at him, expressing a lot of resentment, being cold and distant, saying cutting things that I know will hurt him. I tear him down when I talk about him to my children. I try to make him wrong. I want them to see him as cruel, disloyal. I want them to hate him and side with me.

Who would you be without the thought that your husband should come back?

I would be free of all that.

"My husband should come back to the family"—turn it around.

I should come back to the family. Yes, my children have probably been missing me even more than they miss him—even though I'm there. And I miss them. We could be having so much fun together.

Nothing can cost you someone you love. The only thing that can cost you your husband is if you believe a thought. That's how you move away from him. That's how the marriage ends. You are one with your husband until you believe the thought that he should look a certain way, he should give you something, he should be something other than what he is. That's how you divorce him. Right then and there you have lost your marriage.

Is there another turnaround?

I should come back to myself.

Feel it. That is the healing.

Yes. It feels as though I have been away and there's been nobody home. Now it feels like opening the front door and coming back in. I could be a happy woman, a happy divorced woman.

Can you find one more turnaround?

I should come back to him.

Can you see it?

Yes.

No one can keep you from loving him; you're the only one who can. You've been believing stories that keep you from the awareness of love, the great love in you for your husband and children, so that you pretend that you don't want him to be happy. I can close my eyes and see my husband in the arms of a woman loving him, and I want that if it's what he wants, and I also see my life without him and how full that would be. I always have an abundance of love in my life. Everyone does. There's never a shortage and never too much. The way we know that this Work is alive in us is when we find ourselves, without a plan, living the turnarounds. "I should come back to the family, and I should come back to myself, and I should come back to him." And you go home, and you call your husband and tell him, "I love you, and I am so happy you're with this woman. I've been looking inside me, and this is what I found, and I am so touched by this love I feel for you." The belief about your husband was nothing more than an attempt to keep you from the awareness of the love that you are.

My Teacher Let Me Down

I'm angry at the woman who used to be my spiritual teacher because she taught me to renounce the world and my family, and to do spiritual practices in order to get God's grace. But after I devoted my life to serving her and gave her all my money, she didn't help me when I needed help.

"She didn't help you"—is that true?

There were many times when she didn't help me. And there are times when I can say "Yes, she did help me." But I still can't get rid of the times that the anger comes up, and I feel—

Let's slow it down, sweetheart, let's move back to inquiry. Just answer yes or no. "She didn't help you"—is that true?

No.

Settle into that, allow the mind to take it in. We don't like to hear the truth. It opposes what we believe. The mind's job is to run away from the questions and prove that what it believes is right. It's like a frightened child. So, sweetheart, how does it feel when you believe the thought "She took all my money and didn't help me"?

I get very upset, disappointed, and I feel like she ruined my life.

Yes, honey. Who would you be without the thought "She didn't help me"?

In a much more peaceful place. I wouldn't be so angry.

Yes. So, "She didn't help me"—turn it around.

I didn't help me.

Does that seem as true or truer?

Yes. It's truer.

Now find three genuine ways that you didn't help you.

I don't understand.

Did she make you stay?

No.

So that's one reason. Did you help yourself when you stayed with her, even though you were unhappy?

No, I didn't. Oh, I see. And she didn't make me give her all my money either. She said it would be good for me to do that.

Good. So that's two. You gave her your money, and you gave it with reservations, and when you did that you weren't helping yourself.

That's true. And the third one is that I gave up my family.

Good, sweetheart. Did she make you do that?

I have to say no. She didn't force me to do anything.

You did all that because you wanted something from her. What was it?

I wanted God's grace. And I thought I could get it by doing the spiritual practices she recommended—like cutting off my family and giving her all my money. I thought she'd approve of me if I did all that.

"You can earn God's grace by winning her approval"—
is that true?

*Well, now that I know that she's not really a spiritual person, no,
it's not true.*

"Some people are more spiritual than others"—can
you know that that's true?

At this point I have my doubts. No, I can't know that.

How do you react when you believe that thought?

*I feel like I'm not a spiritual person. I used to run around trying to
be calm and humble, doing whatever I could to please the most
spiritual person I could find. I pretended not to be angry when I
was. It was a lot of effort.*

"I'm not spiritual, so I'll act spiritual."

Right. I thought I had to work really hard for it.

So who would you be, living your life without the
belief that some people are more spiritual than others?

I'd have a lot of free time.

And a lot more money.

*I wouldn't be constantly trying to be like someone else. I guess I'd
just get on with what was in front of me to do.*

That sounds spiritual. And free. Maybe freedom is just
an ordinary, happy woman. I invite my children to
make friends with being ordinary. It's a very nice place
to be. I'm not more than or less than—I'm just me. It's
a wonderful thing to be what I am anyway. I've always
been just me, but I was the last to know that it was all
right.

I wish I could feel that way.

So, "You need to get someone else's approval to have God's grace"—is that true?

No, it couldn't be.

"You need to get God's grace"—is that true?

I want God's grace, but I don't think I could ever be good enough to get it.

What would you have if you had God's grace?

I'm not sure. I think it would be like being in a state of grace myself. Everything would seem perfect—but I can't really imagine it.

And how would you feel if you had your teacher's approval?

Right now it wouldn't mean anything to me, but then it would have meant the world. It would have been such bliss.

Like God's grace?

What? Oh. That's true. They were the same in my thoughts. Both of them were supposed to take away my unhappiness.

So, "I need God's grace"—how do you react when you believe that thought?

Unhappy. I feel unworthy and desperate, as though I were cast out of heaven and would do anything to get in.

Including giving up your family and giving all your money to your teacher?

Right. That's exactly what I felt.

Oh, my! Sweetheart, here's how I get God's grace: I put this teacup down, and then I pick it up. This is perfection and total approval from all directions. I'm so grateful to be sitting here with you, holding this cup. I can't imagine anything better. Who would you be without the thought that you need God's grace?

I'd be right here smiling at you, just the way I am. What a fool I've been!

And who are you without the thought that you've been a fool?

My smile gets bigger.

Yes, you get to be a holy fool. Everything you've done, your whole past, was necessary for you to come here and have that smile. Just stay for a while with the experience that brought it to you, the state of being you without the thought that you need to seek anything. It's the grace of God. No one can give you that or take it away. Only uninvestigated thoughts can take it away, thoughts like "I have to earn God's grace" and thoughts about how your teacher made you do things. How could that be? She didn't make you stay. You stayed for love. If I had a prayer, it would be this: "God spare me from the desire for love, approval, and appreciation. Amen." So, "I need God's grace"—can you turn that around?

I don't need God's grace?

How can you need what you already have? I love that you're beginning to see that, sweetheart.

7

WHAT IF MY PARTNER IS FLAWED?

❧

Some people ask if The Work advocates passive acceptance of one's relationship, however bad it is. I tell them that The Work doesn't advocate anything. How can it? It's just four questions and a turnaround. It's sometimes hard for people to hear this. "If I love my partner just as he is," they say, "doesn't this mean accepting his flaws and staying with him? Why should I put up with him? What if he really is flawed?" What an interesting question this is. Let's take a look.

"He's so inconsiderate: he tracks mud into the house, he sits on my freshly made bed to tie his shoes in his dirty work pants, he doesn't hear what I say because he's focused on the football game." "She snores." "She doesn't do it right." "He threw the whites in the washing machine with the red socks and now the whites are forever pink." "She stopped exercising and gained weight: just look at her in that tight dress!" "He's heading out the door on the way to a job interview all dressed up and with dried egg in his beard."

Why do these things happen? It may not be clear at first. But if you take a minute, you'll discover that they're wonderful ways of bringing us closer together. Not if you're passive, though. This is about your own empowerment, your ability to see things as they really are, through the eyes of love. When you do The Work on your partner, you realize that all your problems are coming from you, because it's your thoughts that are telling you who he is. If you see him as flawed in any way, you can be sure that you've found a place where you're arguing with reality in that moment and are blind to yourself. (One way to find such places is to notice where you feel most righteous and justified in your attack.) Go back to the source; go to yourself.

Let's look at the husband with egg in his beard. You can see him in two ways. First, when you think he's flawed: "Oh God, there he goes with egg in his beard! Hey, stop! You have egg in your beard! What a slob! I don't know what you're thinking of— wash it off! Hurry, you're late! Here, let me do that, you've had your chance. Why do I have to point these things out to you? They'll never give you that job. You can be so frustrating—why did I even marry you? No, stop it, I don't want to kiss you. Just leave me alone and get out of here."

The other way is when you know that being flawed is simply not possible: "He's going out the door with egg in his beard. That is so funny—he must be in a big rush, to have missed something so obvious. I'll wipe the egg off for him as I notice a few of the rea-sons this happened for us, or at least for me. It happened so that I could see his beard in time to save the day, of course. So that we could laugh together as we imagine what the job interview could have looked like with egg in his beard. I get to wipe off the egg for him, and that is warm and dear and funny and intimate. I didn't think I had time to kiss him goodbye and the dried egg made it possible. (Interesting how time opens up when you think there's no time.) And I get the credit for his new job!"

"I'm Sick and Tired of Living with His Flaw"—An Inquiry

My husband is always late. It has been an issue for him since childhood. He agrees, his mother agrees, I agree—and it's driving me nuts. He's uncaring, inconsiderate, undependable, inept, and a poor example for our children. I'm just sick and tired of living with someone who doesn't care enough to change.

Okay. Suppose you're right. What can you do? You've been trying to get him to change for twenty years, and it hasn't worked. How about questioning these things in your own mind? After all, you're the one who is miserable. "He's always late"—turn it around.

But I'm never late. This turnaround doesn't work.

Is that true? Can you think of three times in your life when you've been late? You might find them in areas that aren't the same as his.

Well, I was what they call a "late bloomer"—I was very slow at school. Later on I turned out to excel at music and mathematics.

What was that like?

It was awful when my parents and teachers got on my case about being so slow. I always knew I'd get there eventually, but they didn't. I think their judgments about me slowed me down, I was so ashamed.

Any other ways?

I don't always pay our bills on time.

One more?

Once or twice I've put things off to the last minute and it causes a lot of anxiety in me and I have to rush the others to compensate.

"He is uncaring, inconsiderate, a poor example for our children"—how might you turn that around?

I'm inconsiderate when I yell at him about being late; I don't really care about him in those moments. And I don't consider how that makes him feel. And it is a poor example to our children when they see that I deal with the situation by yelling at someone I love.

And no wonder you're sick and tired of living with someone who doesn't care enough to change. That person is you. And there's no release or escape from yourself until you leave him alone and focus on your own turnarounds. Changing him will no longer be your life's work. You can be your life's work. You're the one who believes in change.

I just can't imagine how I could deal with his lateness differently.

His lateness is his business. You might just take care of your own. For instance, you could stop waiting for him to be on time. Let's think of a worst-case situation. What's the worst thing you can imagine his being late for?

Our only daughter is getting married this June, and he's supposed to be giving her away. If he's late for the wedding, I don't know what I'll do.

Let's try it out. You play the role of your daughter on her wedding day, and her father is late. I'll be the honest wife who loves him unconditionally, I'll be you. He's running late, and we're at the wedding. *[Katie speaking as mother]* Hi, honey. What a wonderful day to get married! You look beautiful.

[Mother speaking as daughter] Where's Dad?

Oh, he's running late, sweetheart.

What do you mean? It is time to start now!

I know it. What do you suggest? I could walk you down the aisle if you like.

Don't be ridiculous, Mom! Couldn't you do anything with him?

No, honey. I just know that he's doing the best that he can. I offered to help and he said to leave him alone.

And what did you do?

I honored what he wanted, of course.

Mom, that was so the wrong thing to do. You should have pushed him. It's my wedding! Oh God, now he won't make it! It's all your fault!

I hear that, sweetheart, and what can we do to make it right at this point? You look so beautiful, even though a little panicked.

Look at what you imagine is a flaw in your partner, and notice the ways that it gives you an opportunity to appreciate him or her. If you can't find these ways, you'll eventually have to strike out in anger—or you may just become frustrated at your lack of progress and attack yourself and her mentally. These attacks that you experience along the way are simply areas that need to be questioned, that's all. If the ways become obvious, you'll grow and grow into love without limit.

Well, I'm desperate! Okay, will you walk me down the aisle?

Yes, honey. It would be an honor. Is it okay if I cry?

What for, Mom?

I've never been so grateful as this for your father's lateness. I get to walk my daughter down the aisle! I love
you both so much that I could just pop!

Mom, you're the greatest! Oh, there he is now! Dad! Hurry!

What a story, honey! How could we ever believe that
he'd be late at all? How could we believe that "late" is
even possible? He's obviously coming at the perfect
time. Now I get to sit and watch the wedding of my
daughter's dreams, with her father giving her away,
and nothing could be better than that.

A Really Bad Relationship—with Whom?

The Work is never passive, though its results are always peaceful.
Sometimes you may find yourself in a relationship with someone
who is angry, hurtful, physically aggressive, or unkind toward
himself, someone who projects his thoughts onto you and really
believes that you are the cause of his suffering. Get out of the relationship, by all means, if that's what seems right to you. A bad relationship is a different story with the same answer: Ask yourself.

If I live with someone who projects his thoughts onto me to
the point that my body is bruised or broken, I need to question
my beliefs. I need to question the thoughts that have frightened
me into staying. And I need to question statements like "He
shouldn't hit me or shout at me or withhold from me" and turn

them around: "I shouldn't hit me, using his hands to do it. I shouldn't shout at me in my mind. I shouldn't withhold (happiness) from me." Is that as true or truer? And if it is, how might I live these turnarounds?

Leaving or Staying, in Peace

You may or may not be willing to put up with your partner's apparent flaws. Whether you stay in or leave a relationship, there are always two ways to do it. One way is in peace, with love; the other is at war, with anger and blame. If you want to be in peace, judge your partner, write it down, ask four questions, and turn it around. Clearly see that his flaws are flaws in your own vision. Then let the decision make itself. It always happens right on time, and not one second before.

I am devoting the rest of this chapter to the following conversation with a woman from Amsterdam because it's a perfect example of how someone can believe a thought so thoroughly that it seems like a fact. This woman was absolutely convinced that her husband was terminally uncommunicative and that she was going to leave him. But when she inquired into these apparent facts, they turned out to be just two more unquestioned thoughts.

Welcome, sweetheart. Let's hear what you've written.

I wrote about my marriage because I'm going to leave my husband, and I feel a lot of guilt about it.

"You're going to leave him"—is that true?

Yes.

Can you absolutely know that it's true?

It's not your job to understand
me—it's mine.

In this moment? No, I guess not.

How do you react when you believe that thought, "I'm going to leave him"?

I feel a lot of guilt.

How do you treat him when you believe that thought and feel guilty?

I get angry at him.

Yes, it's as if you've already left him. You leave him emotionally. Who would you be without the thought that you're going to leave your husband? Let's say you're going to leave in five days. During those five days, living with that man, who would you be without the thought?

Peaceful. I think I would see him as more of a whole person.

Yes, when you see him without guilt, you could have a nice time. He might even help you pack.

I would like that.

And you could both wish you well. "I'm going to leave him"—turn it around.

I'm not going to leave him.

Can you find three ways that you're not going to leave him, even if you move out?

I still care about him. I'll invite him to see the children on a regular basis. I will be there if he needs me.

Yes, you could be really good friends. It's wonderful to love and care about the father of your children. That is a gift of an open mind. When your mind is open, your heart is open. You can't have one without the other. Parents who separate and believe what they think can be cold, angry, and confused. It doesn't leave much experience of the heart. People can love each other without condition and still get divorced. We don't have to leave in anger.

But it seems harder when there is love, because I think I don't have a motivation to leave.

"You have to have fear or hate as a motivator"—is that true?

No. I see that it isn't. Still, it's easier to explain to other people if there are a lot of arguments and anger.

Let's just work with your own understanding. How do you explain to yourself why you're leaving?

I'm leaving him because he doesn't want to talk to me.

Okay, so here's how you explain it to people. When they ask why you're leaving him, you can say, "I love him with all my heart, and I want to live with someone who talks to me."

Oh.

And when your husband asks, "Why are you leaving me?" you can say, "Because you don't talk to me." You have your reason. It may not be good enough for the rest of the world, but it's good enough for you. When you're at peace with your reason, your mind isn't a war zone. You stop teaching your children that the way to leave is in anger. You can teach another way. You have your reason to leave, and you still love him, and you love yourself for being balanced and caring. What did you write down next?

I'm angry at my husband because he let me and our marriage down.

"He let the marriage down"—is that true?

I'm not really sure.

When you do this Work, yes and no are equally good answers. Or you can say, "I don't know." "He let the marriage down"—is that true?

No, it's not.

I hear your answer is no. Where did you find the no?

I got a bit dizzy in the head. I'm not clear about who's at fault anymore.

Good. So for now it's a no. How do you react when you believe the thought "He let the marriage down"?

I remember how I fought for our marriage, and I think he should have listened to me. When he walks into the room, my thoughts begin to attack him, finding all the ways he is letting the marriage down. I push him away with my energy.

When he walks into the room, who would you be if you didn't believe that he let the marriage down?

I would see a man walking into a room, and it would be okay.

Yes, you'd just be available, whether he has anything to say or not. And even if he is silent, you could watch him without finding fault with him. So, "He let the marriage down"—turn it around.

I let the marriage down.

Can you find three ways you let the marriage down?

Let's see . . . I criticize him a lot. I want more from the relationship than I let him know. I push him too much.

You may want to share this with him: "Sweetheart, I let the marriage down and I'm sincerely sorry for that." And then you can tell him specifically what you just found. Let's look at your next statement.

I need my husband to understand that I can't be in the marriage any longer.

"You need him to understand"—is that true?

I would like him to.

"You *need* him to understand"—can you absolutely know that that's true? This is a very important question.

No, I can't absolutely know that.

How do you react when you believe the thought that you need him to understand, and he doesn't?

I keep looking for something that I can't have. I keep looking over there all the time, at him. I keep looking to him for answers, and he doesn't have any, and I get more and more frustrated.

How do you treat him when he still doesn't give you understanding?

I treat him as if it's his fault.

And when he still doesn't understand?

I give up.

What does that look like, when you give up, and you still think you need him to understand?

I become patronizing and bitter, or quiet and sulky. I feel and behave like a victim.

Who would you be without that thought, "I need him to understand"?

Relieved of a lot of stress. Allowing him to be who he is in his silence.

Even when people say, "Oh, I understand," we can never be sure what it is they're understanding. This is impossible, honey. Let's look at what's possible. "I need him to understand me"—turn it around.

I need to understand myself.

Yes, you've given yourself a lot of understanding just by writing out this Worksheet. Whenever you want to understand yourself, judge your partner, write it down, ask four questions, and turn it around. Can you find another turnaround for "I need my husband to understand me"?

I need to understand my husband.

It could be that he is hurting and *can't* understand. You have some answers for him now, answers that you can give him in a loving way, without anger. Let him know what you've been discovering about yourself, as you would a good friend. And then understand him. There's another turnaround.

I don't need him to understand me. That would be nice.

If we are clear and honest, it's much simpler for the people who love us to understand where we're coming from. We're not screaming at them as if they are enemies. We're just kind and loving, and we let them know clearly how *we* have contributed to the problem. We know that they want to understand, but if we expect any understanding from them, we're off the mark. What's important is not that they understand, it's that we understand. Because this is where we are the happiest.

That feels much better, because then I am responsible for the situation.

Read the next statement you wrote.

My husband shouldn't let me down by not talking to me.

Turn it around.

I shouldn't let me down by not talking to myself.

Yes. Are you looking for answers from him that are within you?

They're hard to find.

And you think he should be able to do it. Read the next statement.

I need my husband to see where I am now.

"You need him to see where you are now"—is that true?

I would like that. It would make me more calm and secure.

Let's look at it this way: "He doesn't see where you are now"—is that true? Have you told him that you're leaving?

No.

"Your husband should see where you are now"—is that true?

No.

That's a good find. You've been silent.

I have talked about everything leading up to this point.

And "He should see where you are *now*"—is that true? Is he psychic?

No.

How do you react when you believe that thought, and he has no clue that you're leaving him?

I get very stressed.

Turn it around.

My husband should not see where I am now.

It's not possible. Why are you afraid of telling him?

I'm afraid that he'll go into shock and fall apart.

You're afraid that he'll go into shock and fall apart, and then what will happen to you?

I'll feel responsible and have huge guilt. And I'm afraid of the anger of Grandma, my mother-in-law, and all that.

Okay, let's play it out. You be your husband, and I'll be someone who loves him very much: I'll be your honest self. *[Katie speaking as wife]* Sweetheart, I've made up my mind to leave you.

[Wife speaking as husband] You can't. It's not possible.

I hear that, and I'm leaving.

But you have to give our marriage a try.

I have. It's very strange. I love you so much, and I'm leaving.

But you have to try harder. There are ups and downs in every relationship.

That's true. You're doing very well with this.

I am?

That's how I see it. I thought you would be shocked and fall apart when I told you, but you're still standing there talking to me. *[Katie as herself]* Okay, now be the grandmother, the one you're so afraid of.

[Wife speaking as Grandma] You are so spoiled. Think of all the things you have, and everything he's done for you. You're only thinking of yourself.

You know, you're right. He *has* done so many wonderful things for me, and he *is* such a wonderful father. He's amazing. I really love him.

Then why are you leaving him?

Because he's silent. He doesn't talk to me.

But think of the children. Think of how much they will suffer.

You could be right. I'm going to be as kind and generous as I can be. I want them to know what a wonderful father they have.

So stay with him!

I'm not able to do that. He doesn't talk to me. *[Katie as herself]* Sweetheart, you've questioned your thoughts now. You know what is true for you, you know how loving and caring he is, and you know how loving and caring you are. You know how much everyone cares about the children. You have everything you need in order to be an honest human being. No one ever has to be afraid of the truth. It's the defenses that we build around the truth that strike fear into our hearts. When I spoke for you, everything I said came from what you wrote on your Worksheet. Let's look at your next statement.

My husband is closed, stubborn, keeps his thoughts to himself, he's innocent, special, hysterical, angry, and hectic.

Turn it around: "I am . . ."

I am closed.

So, find out where you are closed. For one thing, you haven't told him you're leaving. Where else are you closed with your husband, your children, yourself? You're leaving him anyway, so you may as well open up to this man. Who knows, you may meet somebody you've never met before. The truth can change a lot of things. Read the next one.

I am stubborn. I do tend to stick to my ideas.

Yes. For instance, his silence could be a wonderful thing for you. "What do you want for dinner, sweetheart?" Silence. "Good, then I don't have to cook. Is there anything you'd like to do this weekend?" Silence. "When you find out, just let me know." And you just move on with your plans, with your life. "Do you love me?" Silence. Well, I can just look around the house and answer that. I look at the children, and I see he loves me. I look at the photos, and I see he loves me. The walls? He loves me. The floor? He loves me. How blind am I that I have to ask him? And then you can say to him, honestly, "I love you," if that's true for you. Read the next one.

I am innocent.

Yes, honey, you are innocent. Look at all the things you believed that are not even true for you. That's innocence.

And I'm trying my best.

Yes, every single human being is trying his best. We're all doing the best we can. But when we believe what we think, we have to live out those thoughts. When there's chaos in our heads, there's chaos in our lives. When there's hurt in our thinking, there's hurt in our lives. Love thy neighbor as thyself? I always have. When I hated me, I hated you. That's how it works. If I hate someone, I'm mistaking them for me, and solutions remain hidden. Let's look at the next one.

I am hectic and angry.

It's more accurate to say, "My *thinking* is hectic and angry." And you're learning how to take care of that by questioning it. Read the next one.

I never ever want to have the experience again that my husband doesn't want to talk to me.

Turn it around.

It's okay that my husband doesn't want to talk to me. I look forward to my husband not wanting to talk to me.

So now you be your silent husband, and I'll be someone who loves him. I'll be you. *[Katie speaking as wife]* Hi, sweetheart. Will you talk to me?

[Wife speaking as husband] Do I have to?

Wow! You're talking! And no, you don't have to. You never have to. I'm so grateful.

Good. I'm grateful too.

What would you like for dinner?

Hmm, I don't know.

Okay, until you know, I'm just going to feed the children.

That sounds nice.

Good. You're so easy to live with!

Thank you.

You're welcome. How was your day today?

Hmm. Stressed, but it's okay now.

That's great. You are amazing! You really worked through it.

Yes, I guess I did.

You know, you are just one peaceful guy. What were you stressed about?

Oh, it was just someone not doing his job. You know, stuff like that.

Can I sit on your lap?

What? Right now?

Yes, right now. Can I sit on your lap and put my arms around you?

Yes, that's okay. Come on.

[Katie breaks off the role-playing] Are you realizing that this guy is answering every question I ask?

Yes. You're right.

So now you know you're not leaving him because he's silent. You're just leaving him.

Maybe that's right. Shit! Is it possible?

To keep your reason for leaving—the thought that he doesn't talk to you—you have to believe it even while he's talking to you. That's how powerful a belief is. I noticed that he answered every question. He just sounded tired.

Yes, he works hard.

I don't see a problem here. Listen to the way he answered you. Maybe if you approached him in a different way he would be excited. He doesn't say anything, and you keep believing what you think. He answers every question, plus this guy is low maintenance. Even when he has a rough time at work, he works it out before he comes home. He doesn't mind if you make dinner or not. That could give you a very pleasant life.

Yes, but in a way I feel I did a better job answering than he would have. And I don't know if I could be as loving as you were without his answers.

Very good. So, have you tried just asking him about his life? Maybe *you* are the quiet one. What do you want to talk to him about?

I want to talk about our relationship, of course.

So you could say, "Sweetheart, what do you think about our relationship?"

Not in those words. I say things like, "I'm very sorry that we can't talk about things, that we don't communicate." Okay, Katie, I can hear the problem.

Good. So you have the thought that he's silent, and believing that, you walk up to him and say, "You never talk to me. What's the matter with you? We don't have anything in common." There's not much room for discussion in that. And if he really cares about you and doesn't want to see you upset, he might think that he'd better not argue with you. That could make him pretty quiet. So when you go home, notice how you communicate with him. It could be that he's silent because of the way you communicate. It could be that you're approaching him that way, and he doesn't want to upset you.

Yes, that could be true.

Okay, precious, nice Work. I see why he loves you. Now that you see that you have nothing to be afraid of, if you feel confused, just continue to judge your husband. Don't stop—write down more reasons for leaving or for staying. None of them is a "fact," and none can make an enemy of your husband. And you don't have to be afraid of the grandmother. It's unnecessary because it sounds like she loves you and her grandchildren.

Under inquiry, this dear woman's reason to leave didn't hold up. She may have ended up leaving or staying in her marriage, but she saw that she didn't have to stop loving her husband. When you question what you think, you may see that love was always there but you were blind to it. If I think, "What's the matter with him?" there is something the matter with *me* in that moment. I've just put an obstacle between us. It's only a thought, but look what my mind does with it. And until I question what I believe about him, until I do The Work, I lose the awareness of love. So I question it, and then love is visible again. If I don't love you, I've lost my sanity. I'm out of touch with myself; I'm out of touch with what gives me the greatest happiness. So I question any stressful belief that I have about you and turn it around, and then love lives—the awareness of love lives. But the questioning has to be the real thing. I have to go inside myself and find genuine answers, answers that are true for me. When I find what is true for me, there are no obstacles anymore. There are no barriers between me and my partner, or between me and anyone in the world.

When you own your share in something that your partner did to you, it's the sweetest thing in the world. You just feel humility, without the slightest urge to defend yourself. It leaves you completely vulnerable. This is the kind of vulnerability you want to lick off the plate, it's so delicious.

8

FIVE KEYS TO FREEDOM
IN LOVE

☙

In the following pages you'll find some ways to support yourself and hold your own hand while you question what may seem unquestionable.

Matching Socks

Let's look at a familiar example of what people often feel as a desperate need. Your thought is "I need her to come back to me," and she has made it very clear that she isn't coming back to you. When you ask yourself, "Is it true that I need her to come back to me?" try these prompting questions: "Is this what I really need? Can I know what is ultimately best for me? Am I going on with my life? Am I still breathing? Did I put on two socks today? Do they match?" These questions will gently bring you back to the reality of the life you're living very well in this moment, without her, even while you're thinking that you can't go on without her, that you *need* her to come back to you. They help you put to rest the childlike thought that your survival is at stake. The child says, "Who cares if my socks match when I have a broken heart?" Your answer is: Apparently *you* care. The proof is on your feet. This is very important to notice.

The word *need* suggests a permanent state of mind. When you think, "I need her to come back to me," you believe that you'll always be feeling that way. But if you look at your experience clearly, you'll see that there aren't any permanent states of mind. How many of your problems today come from believing a thought about the future? In the moment when you think that you need love, you're imagining future moments in which you'll think that you need love. You literally imagine yourself sitting, standing, or lying down somewhere five years from now and thinking, "I need her to love me." It's a very painful thought.

Scaring yourself with that thought is easy: All you have to do is believe it. Unscaring yourself is just as easy; you can do it in a few moments as you sit in your living room with your matching socks. First notice the conjuring trick. Realize that you're summoning up that future in your thoughts. See how you're devoting this actual moment to that made-up future. Ask yourself the four questions about your assumption of what will happen in some future moment. "'Six months or five years from now I'll need her to come back to me'—is that true? Can I absolutely know that it's true? Can I even know that I'll want her? How do I react when I believe that thought? Who would I be without it?" Then turn the thought around, and find three reasons why each turnaround may be as true or even truer. Options come quickly to an open, fearless mind.

Once a painful concept is met with understanding, the next time it appears you may find it interesting. What used to be the nightmare is now just interesting. The next time it appears, you may find it funny. The next time, you may not even notice it. This is the power of loving what is.

You Can Make It Without Your Fear

Some thoughts seem too frightening to examine. Thoughts like "I couldn't make it without you" or "If my children died, I couldn't go on living" can terrify you, and then, instead of asking if you really believe them, you might push them back down or live as if they were true and, as a result, feel anxious without knowing why. This section explores some of the reasons you might block your own inquiry.

Most people have someone or something in their lives that they think they couldn't make it without. You might take all kinds of precautions to avoid losing your husband, your child, your money, your job, your home. Usually the precautions include worrying a lot and placing limitations on the people you love, trying to keep them out of the trouble you're afraid of.

Sometimes reality steps in and takes away what people think they couldn't bear losing. In fact, they survive. When the worst thing that could happen has happened, people will tell you (if you dare to ask) that living with the fear of it was more painful than the actual event. Often their friends and relatives had a bigger problem with the event than they did. Here is one woman's experience:

> When my mother was dying of pancreatic cancer, I lived in her bedroom and slept beside her for four weeks, until she died. I fed her and bathed her and dispensed her drugs, I cooked for her and cherished her. Her breath became my rhythm. We plucked our eyebrows and painted our nails, and we laughed and laughed. We talked about everything that was important to her, and we watched Oprah together. I never had a sweeter time with my mother. When people visited with their stories of how terrible it was that she was dying, I watched her become a cancer victim before my

very eyes. She seemed to think it was expected of her. Everyone would be solemn and sad and hushed, until the moment the door closed behind the visitors, and my mother and I would go right back to normal—receiving, giving, crying, and laughing and laughing.

People who live through it will tell you that their experience of loss was kinder than their beliefs about how it would be. Inquiry allows you to take the fear out of loss *before* anything happens to those you love. It also reveals the harm that fearful beliefs do to your relationships when everybody is still around and doing just fine in reality. And there is a huge benefit for the people close to you when they see that you realize that your life doesn't depend on their welfare. If you don't need them to stay alive for your sake, they are free to live for themselves.

"IF MY CHILDREN DIED, I COULDN'T GO ON LIVING"—IS IT TRUE?

This is a thought that most people can relate to, even if they don't have children. The automatic response from many parents, especially parents of young children, is "Yes, of course it's true. If my child died, I wouldn't be able to bear it."

What are the related thoughts that might block you from finding a genuine answer, or from even questioning that thought? Here is one that you may have: "I'd be a traitor to my children if I even considered that I *could* go on living without them. It would mean that I don't really love them." This thought is, of course, completely insane, but that never stopped anyone from believing it. The craziness is easier to see when the thought is rephrased more simply: "If I don't live in fear of losing my children, it means that I don't love them" or "If I don't suffer, it means that I don't care." And sometimes the mind goes even further. Like superstitious cavemen, people may believe "If I allowed myself to think I could survive something terrible, that terrible event would happen." Thoughts like this do have power, but their power is of a different kind. The next question reveals precisely what effect they have.

HOW DO YOU REACT WHEN YOU BELIEVE THAT THOUGHT?

How do you live when you believe that if your children died, you couldn't go on living? How do you treat your children when you believe that thought? You probably restrict them and try to keep them safe in ways that may not be healthy for them. You also treat them as if your life depended on them, because according to that thought it does. This means that you treat your children as if they existed for your sake. "Sweetheart, don't run into the street, because I don't think I could go on living if you died." When you act like this, what are you teaching them? That the world is a frightening place and that something terrible may happen at any moment. You're also teaching them that it's their job to keep you alive and that they're responsible for you. And how do you treat yourself when you believe that thought? You fill your mind with fear and worry. You constrict your heart. You impose upon yourself an imagined future of sheer pain. You are never just present with yourself, because your thoughts can't leave your children alone.

WHO WOULD YOU BE WITHOUT THAT THOUGHT?

Who would you be as a loving parent, raising your children, if you were incapable of even thinking the thought "If my children died, I couldn't go on living"? Take your time with this question. Feel the effect of taking terror out of your relationship with your children. It leaves you with love. It leaves you showing your children how to cross the street confidently, intelligently, how to take good care of themselves for their own sake, not yours. Following your example, they might come to see that if someone they loved died, they would make it—they'd be just fine.

TURN THE THOUGHT AROUND.

"If my children died, I *could* go on living." Don't be halfhearted here. Ask yourself to imagine what you think is unimaginable: the life you *could* lead without your children. Be a traitor to misery and find some advantages to that life. There's nothing macabre about this. The point is to break the grip of a fearful belief. Find three ways in which your life would be better without your children. (The move here is a powerful, all-purpose lifesaver: Whenever you think you couldn't bear something, find three proofs that you could in reality bear it.) It doesn't matter if these three ways seem silly, as long as they are genuine. "I could have the first shower in the morning." "I could go to the movies and not hire a sitter." "I could become the schoolteacher I always wanted for them."

You may think that these reasons are ridiculously light when balanced against having your children in your life. But you're not weighing one thing against the other. All you're doing here is meeting your terror with something more honest: "If my children died, I *could* go on living." And then you can come back to reality in a new way.

Imagine your child coming up to you and asking, "Mom, would you be okay without me?" Now you can look into his or her eyes and say, "I love you in my life, and I'd really miss you. And I would be fine."

"Really, Mom? What would you do without me?"

"Well, sweetheart, let me see. I wouldn't have to get up so early in the morning, and I'd have the first shower, and I could go out whenever I liked. And the bottom line is that I love you in my life. Nothing can take you out of my heart, honey, ever." There's no fear there. You've learned—and they learn—that love doesn't mean fear.

This Moment *Should* Be Happening

One way to be miserable and confused is to conjure up a long-term need. ("I may be okay right now, but I'll need a husband by next year.") Another way is to believe thoughts that object to the present moment. The two have a lot in common. In both cases you're living in thoughts that separate you from what is; you're arguing with reality instead of enjoying or simply dealing with it.

A friend of a friend of mine was working on a construction crew in the middle of a Michigan winter. It was a blustery fifteen-degree day, and the wind tore a large sheet of plywood off the roof. It landed on one of the workers, along with a load of snow. The rest of the crew watched the carpenter as he got to his feet, brushing off the snow and checking himself for damage. They were expecting a burst of foul language. Instead, the carpenter said, "I like it like this," and began to laugh. The other workers lost all control, rolling around with laughter, tears freezing on their cheeks. Nothing better could have happened.

What does this story have to do with love? It *is* love.

The opposite of love might be those moments when you are completely disgusted with what is happening, when you have a fit of total rejection, shock, or regret. Everybody knows what is usually the last word on the black-box flight recorder recovered after a plane crash. It's the same word you might say when you've locked your keys inside your car and you're late for a meeting, or right after someone cancels a date at the last minute.

Many people's lives are constantly punctuated with little fits or tantrums in which they express their rejection of what's happening. What are the thoughts that come at these moments? "I'm hopeless," "If he hadn't done that . . . ," "She always . . . ," "I knew better than to do this." Many of these thoughts are about what you would have done if you'd known better, or seen it coming, or remembered. You think that if you had done something other than what you did, you could have stayed in control of events. "Oh shit!" marks the point where reality and your plan parted ways. Things don't seem to be going your way, and to the best of your ability you're going to fight reality, even if all you can do is swear, kick a rock, or give someone you love a hard time.

The more you stick to the belief that you're in control, the more of these moments there are in your life. Some people reach a point where they're fighting reality at every step along the way. That's how they react to the thought "I'm calling the shots" when no one seems to be listening. It's a war zone in their minds.

The alternative is to expect reality *not* to follow your plan. You realize that you have no idea what's going to happen next. That way, you're pleasantly surprised when things seem to be going your way, and you're pleasantly surprised when they don't. In the second case, you may not have seen what the new possibilities are yet, but life quickly reveals them, and the old plans don't stop you from moving ahead, from flowing efficiently into the life beyond your schemes and expectations.

Pick your moment: The keys locked in the car. The icy patch where you slipped and broke your leg. The phone message canceling the date you longed for. The moment you found out that he's not coming back. Find the thought that comes with the expletive—"She's breaking up with me," "My life is over"— and ask: "Is it true? Can I absolutely know? How do I react when I believe that? Who would I be, just in this moment, if I didn't believe it?" Then turn it around and allow life to show you the new way to move forward, the way that you haven't seen yet. After some practice you don't have to stand by the phone asking four questions; the questioning becomes a part of you, dissolving stressful thoughts before they can affect you. When your old plan is gone, your mind immediately fills with new possibilities.

You take time off work to meet your girlfriend's flight, and there you are, still standing at the gate after all the passengers have walked by. It takes a few phone calls to figure out that you wrote down the wrong date for her return flight. Apparently the flowers you brought were for a little girl who happens to be standing nearby. The long subway ride home is now free time for you; you pick up a novel you've always wanted to read. You invite a friend over to share the delicious dinner you had so thoughtfully precooked. It's a good day.

The little panics and painful twinges actually disappear when you give your mind this kind of education. It spends less and less time in hopelessness and frustration. Questioning the thought that arises when you hit a bump in your life can radically change the quality of your whole existence.

> We leave the coffee shop and get into the backseat of the car together, a hot cup of coffee in my hand. My husband helps me settle in, smiles at me, puts down the heavy backpack in the space next to me, and bumps into the hand holding the coffee. It spills over my lap and hands. Hot! The clean clothes I put on for work (two hours away and we're running late) are now stained and wet. I keep still and notice a sticky feeling of cream and Sweet'n Low on burned, very wet legs, hands, and fingers. It's okay; the truth is that I'm perfectly fine. I wait to see if blisters begin to rise, and they don't.
>
> He says, "I'm so sorry." He looks shocked. I notice the thought "He knew I was holding hot coffee," and I can see

that if I believed that thought, a burst of anger would arise from it; and as I notice it, the thought immediately and gently sinks back to where it came from. I also notice that the thought is accompanied by the slight smile that comes when you hear a good joke. (I can't know that at the moment when he put down the backpack he was aware of the coffee in my hand, even though he was with me when I bought it.) "He should have remembered that I had coffee in my hand." No, that's not true. I see that I myself can't remember what I don't remember. It's not a possibility. "He doesn't care." How can I know that? And also, how ridiculous! His whole life is about caring. And besides, can you make yourself care in the moment that you don't? Again, not possible.

As we drive along, my mind makes an occasional attempt to comment on the incident and can't find one valid reason to be angry, suffer, resent, attack, or be separate. Once we've mopped up the wetness with some tissues, there is nothing to do but enjoy the scenery of the New England landscape on a beautiful spring day, hold my husband's hand—now that mine is empty—joke around about the coffee spill, smile, and continue our (in my opinion) very pleasant journey.

Noticing and counting the beautiful reasons unexpected things happen for us ends the mystery. If you miss the real reasons, the benevolent reasons that coincide with kind nature, then count on depression to let you know that you missed them. Anger, frustration, and aggressive reasons can always be imagined—and what for? People who aren't interested in seeing why everything is good get to be right. But that apparent rightness comes with disgruntlement, and often depression and separation. Depression can feel serious. So "counting the genuine ways that this unexpected event happened *for* me, rather than *to* me" isn't a game. It's an exercise in observing the nature of life. It's a way of putting yourself back into reality, into the kindness of the nature of things.

"This Is Just What I Needed": The Direct Route to Getting Your Needs Met

It's easy to get totally absorbed in what you think you need in a relationship: "I need you to sit where I can see you. I need you to tell me what you're thinking. I need you to tell me the truth. To never leave me. To trust me. To believe me. To be on time. To keep your promises. To smile. To hold my hand in public. To be more outgoing. To listen to me. To be available. To help me. To marry me. To stay with me. To sleep with me. To give me your money. To nurture me. To agree with me. To see that you're wrong. To know when I want to be alone. To know what I need without having to be told. To be less sensitive. To be more sensitive. To stop being friendly to people I don't like. To be nicer to my friends. To change the music. To love me."

By now your needs are familiar. And you know what the effect is on your life when you believe you're entitled to have them met and it doesn't seem to be happening. The result is a hopeless quest filled with separation, frustration, and resentment. You've seen how to use four questions to ask yourself what you really need in this moment.

There's a direct route to understanding your needs. The direct route is just something to try out. When you're ready, it can be a huge relief, like coming home after a very long journey. And if you're not ready for it, be very gentle with yourself. Stay true to what you think you need. When a need becomes painful, use inquiry to question it, and if it still seems true, ask for it: "I need you to remember my birthday and call me. Please write it down in your Day-Timer." This is living your integrity in that moment.

The direct route is to let reality be the guide to your needs: "What I need is what I have." This is not something to believe;

it's the way things are right now, whether you believe it or not. What does it look like?

How do you know when you don't need people? When they're not in your life. How do you know when you do need them? When they *are* in your life. You can't control the comings and goings of the people you care for. What you *can* do is have a good life whether they come or go. You can invite them, and they come or not, and whatever the result is, that's what you need. Reality is the proof of it.

How do you know you don't need to stand up? You're sitting. Life becomes much simpler this way. How do you know when you need to do something? When you do it. To think that you need to do something when you're not doing it is a lie. It puts you in an uncomfortable position, full of shame, guilt, and frustration. Lying in bed, you chide yourself with the thought, "I need to get up," and you don't. But the truth is that you don't need to get up. Not until you do.

Do you try to motivate yourself with the thought that you need to do something, and end up doing nothing? That would be an interesting discovery. "I need to do it" is just a thought. Try the effect of the turned-around version: "I don't need to do it," and notice that the only time that you need to do something is when you do it. It's a wonderful experiment. Start small: Just lie in bed in peace, unpestered by yourself, until you notice that you're getting up.

You think you need to make a decision? You don't—not until it's made. Afterward you may notice that you didn't actually make the decision: It made itself, right on time, the moment you had all the necessary information. (How do you know you had the information you needed? Because the decision made itself.)

The direct route leaves you needing and loving what's going on in front of you. And what's in front of you keeps expanding until *full* is too small a word.

I am a lover of what is, not because I'm
a spiritual person but because it hurts
when I argue with reality. No thinking
in the world can change it. What is is.
Everything I need is already here now.
How do I know I don't need what I
think I need? I don't have it. So
everything I need is always supplied.

NEEDING CHRISTMAS

Here's an example of needing what you have:

We're spending Christmas in the Caribbean, where everything is supposed to show you a good time. On Christmas Day, my family sets out in search of dinner. My husband is trying to find an upscale place that one of his golfing buddies owns. I am looking for something befitting Christmas. And our son? Anything fun. We wander in the eerily quiet, darkening streets of Cozumel. I'm hurrying my son, who is constantly stopping to count blue and purple Christmas lights in store windows. My husband is leading us in circles, trying to find his friend's place. I'm irritated with both of them and losing hope of finding Christmas.

None of our missions accomplished, family hungry and crabby, we enter a pizza joint. I sit in my plastic chair before a dirty table, utterly disappointed. We wait for our pizza, staring blankly at the TV blaring a Mexican version of MTV.

I sit there nursing the thought "This isn't the Christmas dinner I needed." Meanwhile my husband and son are getting interested in the TV show that is butchering pop songs in Spanish. They start laughing, and I'm infected with their silliness. The pizza comes. It's hot and good. I can't hold on to my thought any longer. And it comes to me: *This is the Christmas dinner I needed. Exactly this.* I realize that nothing could have made me happier than this.

Whose Business Am I in Now?

It's confusing and painful when you try to mind someone else's business. This is especially true when the person whose business you've stepped into is someone you love. Often, you don't realize that you're doing this. Every time you try to second-guess what someone else is thinking or feeling, every time you believe that you know what's good or bad for them, you have moved out of your own business and into someone else's.

For example, your partner looks upset and seems to be avoiding you. She cuts a conversation short and snaps at you. When you ask her what's the matter, she says she doesn't want to talk about it and needs to spend some time alone. Being in her business mentally means worrying about what she is thinking. Can you know what she's thinking or feeling? No. And how do you react when you believe you can? You form theories about it: She's angry at you. She doesn't really love you. You've done something wrong.

How do you treat yourself while you're frightening yourself with these thoughts about her? You put your own life on hold. If she is over there living her life, and you are over there living her life (mentally), there's no one here for you. You neglect yourself and put aside the activities that you enjoy. You make yourself feel separate and lonely, and you think that she's the cause.

And if you believe any one of your theories about her, you might easily act on it. You might find yourself demanding an explanation from her. She said clearly that she wants to be alone, but verifying your theory is more important. Why do you think that? You've been suffering, and you're confused enough to believe that she's the cause of it, so you feel entitled to an explanation from her. Now you are literally, physically, in her business. She gets angry at your intrusion and refuses to talk to you.

In your mind, this only confirms your suspicions. This is the torture chamber of a life lived in someone else's business. And once
you notice this—around her and other people—you may discover that you live there most of the time.

What does it mean to stay in your own business? In this
instance, you would ask yourself who you would be without the
thought that you can know, or need to know, what she's thinking. It would allow you to lead your own life, and to let her lead
hers. And it would allow you to know what your own life is
about, maybe for the very first time.

One of the most loving acts you can do for yourself, and for
everyone else, is to ask, "Right now, in this moment, whose business am I in?" For example, "Whose business is what's bothering
her?" The answer is, obviously, "Her business." "Whose business
is what I feel, and whether I feel loved?" Obviously, "Mine."

There is no more loving way to be with someone than to
stay out of his or her business mentally. What he should do, what
he should feel, whom he should love, how he should see you—all
this is his business, not yours. When you understand this, and
someone tells you, silently or aloud, "Mind your own business" or
"Leave me alone," you can hear it as good advice—as love.

Do you really want to enter the inner room in which someone's feelings are formed? Do you want to control his mind, to
barge in and insert the thoughts and feelings *you* want him to
have? Is it even possible? When you're afraid of what your lover
thinks about you, that is the time to go to your own inner room
and check on your own thinking.

Even when you and your partner are physically close,
you're still living in different worlds, and there is great beauty in
that, the beauty of the unknown yet familiar person you're with.
When you stop believing your theories about your partner, you
return to the reality of your own life. You stand in a solid place

from which you can deeply appreciate her, without the slightest impulse to enter the private room in which her feelings are formed. You get to see who she really is. You get to love her with all your heart and not expect anything in return. When you no longer intrude and have stopped trying to manipulate or control her, you meet someone who is more amazing than anything you could have imagined.

9

THE TRANSFORMATION
OF A MARRIAGE

⚭

The effects on a relationship when both people do inquiry can be nothing short of miraculous. The communication keeps everything open and without secrets. It's not necessary for both partners to do this; if even one does The Work on his or her partner, it will radically change the marriage. But it's more than twice as powerful if both partners do it.

Here's an example. Both partners have written a Worksheet on the other, and each in turn reads the Worksheet aloud. "I'm angry at you, John, because you didn't take out the trash, and the kitchen smells of last night's dinner. I want you, John, to keep your promises. John, you should think of me and consider my nausea and pregnancy. John, you shouldn't be so selfish with your time. John, I need you to carry this baby for a while in your stomach and know how it feels to be sick enough to vomit when you smell last night's dinner in the morning. John, you are uncaring, absentminded, self-centered, unkind, and adorable in this moment."

John's job is to be a listener, to look into her eyes, take her words in, and see if he can find where she is right, without defending or interrupting or justifying. When she has finished reading and he has taken it in, looking into her eyes, he simply says, "Thank you." Then they switch roles and he reads his Worksheet to her. Even if they don't do inquiry on the statements in their Worksheets, this kind of communication can be tremendously healing if each partner really wants to hear what the other thinks and feels. They don't have to do The Work, only be open to listening.

Of course, if they continue by facilitating each other, the experience is even more powerful. The apparent flaws or shortcomings that each sees and dislikes in the other are, after all, the pain that each one feels. When the stressful thoughts are questioned and turned around, she benefits, he benefits, and all the secrets are out in the open. Assumptions are no longer necessary, and when an assumption is made, it is in favor of the other. Not only do these assumptions work, but they feel kind and loving. In a family like this, the awareness of loving what is becomes available in every moment, and conflict disappears. Love, after all, is the power.

What happens in real life when marriage partners bring inquiry into their lives? In this chapter you'll see how a marriage moves from being a disappointing mess, through the stages of inquiry, to arrive at an uncomplicated love. The following story is about a young couple living in Prague. They both use The Work to question their thoughts, independently and together. Here is the woman's account:

My marriage was in chaos and we were spending more and more time apart because we fought so often—almost any conversation might turn into a fight. I was hurt and disappointed every day. I can write about my pain now, but I have to do it from memory, because since then I found inquiry. Those painful fights with my husband never happened again. Isn't that funny? Things shifted so quickly that we were both shocked. I think the best way I can explain what it was like is to tell you the story, showing you some of the inquiry I did and how that changed everything.

Because my neediness caused me so much suffering, I inquired into the thought that I needed my husband's love. I didn't even try to look at whether that thought was true; that seemed too daunting. I just went on to the question about consequences.

"I need my husband's love"—how do I react when I believe that thought? Well, if I believe the thought and my husband smiles at me, there's no problem. But if I can't reach him—he's busy or stressed out or on a business trip—and I believe that I need his love, I feel empty and my stomach contracts. Next, I call him and if I don't reach him, my thoughts run out of control: "Why can't I reach him? Did something happen to him? Is he telling me the truth?" Mixed in with these are judgments: "He is not sensitive enough, he should know when to call." After another hour I panic and think, "I married the wrong man, he doesn't care about me, he never calls when I need him."

When he returns my call in the evening of that day, I treat him like a hostile witness, I cross-examine him. Really I'm waiting for him to say, "I love you," but I don't tell him. And if the words don't come, I say that I'm fed up with his strange and uncaring behavior, and that things can't go on this way. In the aftermath, I feel sad, angry at him and myself, I get a headache and take up smoking again. Instead of sleeping, in my mind I go over everything he told me, and compare it with other things I know, looking for discrepancies. By morning, I need to call him again.

If my husband is at home and he is not in a good mood or busy with some other things and I believe that I need his love, I try to please him at first, and then to talk, even though he has said he's busy. If that doesn't work, I'm disappointed, and I interrupt him, telling him that even when he's at home he's busy, that we need more time for working on our relationship. I remind him of times in the past when he hurt me.

It got so bad that I stopped talking to him and sleeping with him, and I went out when he came home. We stopped cooking and eating together, I let the housework go, didn't wash his clothes anymore, "forgot" to tell him who called for him. The whole thing felt desperately sad and lonely. "I will end up alone like my mother," I thought. "I shouldn't have married him. We're headed for divorce. That other guy who wanted me—I could have chosen him." I criticized every little thing about my husband. Sometimes I took the manipulation so far that I got sick. That worked when I was a kid and people were kind to me, so I thought I'd try it on my husband too. I was worn out from being right and yet I kept escalating the quarrels.

Because I believed so strongly in the thought that I needed my husband's love and couldn't even live without it, my jealousy was a huge problem in our marriage. I hardly went anywhere with my husband, because I felt so terrible when he laughed and had fun with other women—not sexually, just talking, sometimes hugging. And when I did risk a party, we'd go home quarreling. By the end, the fights went on for days, and we took them very, very seriously. It felt like we were fighting to the death.

As I said, I have written all this from memory. It's what I saw when I asked the question "How do I react when I believe the thought 'I need my husband's love'?" Then inquiry came as a kind of gift, and my marriage changed completely. Something else: I was lucky in that my husband and I started practicing it together. Even though inquiry made sense to us from the beginning, we are still amazed that we got to have such a happy marriage. We realize how it happened, but sometimes we're astonished *that* it happened.

I began to seriously question my thoughts—to ask "Is it true?"—when our fights about jealousy became so extreme. First I investigated what happened when I saw him smile at a beautiful woman or talk with her. I thought I knew what it meant. With inquiry, my first surprise was that I couldn't be sure that my thoughts were true. These were the kind of thoughts I would have:

> "He'll leave me."
> "He'll fall in love with her."
> "She is nicer, more intelligent, younger, more beautiful than me."
> "He isn't interested in me."
> "He has forgotten about me."
> "I'm too old, I'm not lovable."
> "He's humiliating me in front of everyone."
> "He is so inconsiderate, he has no loyalty, he's lying to me again."
> "My whole life I've had bad taste in men."
> "My marriage is a farce."
> "I'm a fool to tolerate this."
> "Love always leads to sorrow."

I found out that these painful, painful thoughts were *my* way of torturing myself, not, as I had believed until then, his way of torturing me. That realization knocked my socks off! I had taken these thoughts as self-evident. How could I have been so wrong all these years? And he was still by my side! How was that possible if what I thought about him had been true? It was a completely different way of seeing things.

So after that, I started to go places with him again. I inquired into a thought like "I never want to see him having fun with other women" and turned it around to "I look forward to seeing him having fun with other women." And the very next time that happened, my feelings were different. When he started to talk to another woman, I went over to them and joined the conversation and had fun. Before, I used to run away, and I had always believed that I was lonely because *he* had left *me*.

Of course it wasn't done all at once. But when the old feelings came up again at a party, I went to the bathroom and took out my notebook. Right there, I wrote down my thoughts and inquired into them. When I returned to my own business—which meant looking into *my* thoughts, not his—I felt better immediately. Sometimes he would come looking for me and find me laughing my head off in response to a question like "'He'll leave me for this woman he just got to know'—is it true?" The crazy beliefs that had caused me so much anger and sadness before—suddenly they were no more than a joke I could laugh about.

The same thing happened when my husband was away and I couldn't reach him. I would begin to feel needy again. And then I'd start to inquire: "'He had an accident, he's hurt, he'll die,' 'We'll never meet again,' 'My life will be over'—can I absolutely know that that's true?" Just that was enough to bring peace. The thoughts unraveled as I asked myself the questions. Some beliefs disappeared and I didn't even realize it. I only noticed when we were in situations that would have created endless problems before, and the old feelings didn't arise. Some thoughts needed to be investigated more often, because new variations came up. "I'm not good enough," "Love always causes pain," "People should understand me," "People should keep their promises," "I'm not lovable the way I am," "You have to pay for every second of happiness"—that sort of thing. It seems ridiculous now.

We've been doing inquiry for a year now, and our marriage has changed beyond recognition. We appreciate each other in a calm, peaceful way. If we have a problem with each other, we go to different rooms and write down our thoughts. Then we help each other to inquire. It can be so much fun! Thoughts that had caused a crisis before, that had hurt so much we wanted to break up—today, after half an hour of inquiry, those thoughts pass away like clouds in the summer sky. And our love grows with every misunderstanding we inquire into, with every belief we superimpose upon each other. We actually look forward to bad feelings! And there aren't many of them in our partnership now. Through inquiry we find out that these stories are just telling us where we wandered from the path of love and understanding.

I know now that I'm not a victim. "I need my husband's love"—is it true? How could it be? I'm the only one responsible for my life, my health, my feelings, and my happiness. When my neediness died away, what was left was love. Inquiry has been more than a tool for me; it's been a path to joy and understanding.

Forgiveness is discovering that what you thought happened didn't—that there was never anything to forgive. What seemed terrible changes once you've questioned it. There is nothing terrible except your unquestioned thoughts about what you see. So whenever you suffer, inquire, look at the thoughts you're thinking, and set yourself free. Be a child. Know nothing. Take your ignorance all the way to your freedom.

10

WHAT'S NOT TO LOVE?
COULD IT BE YOU?

⁂

Trying to earn your own love is just as painful as seeking the love of others, and the results are just as unsatisfying. And undoing the search works the same way. When you sincerely question your unexamined thoughts about yourself, love just happens.

In every inquiry about a painful relationship—with your spouse, your mother, or someone at work—you always discover that the stress is caused by your own thinking. It's not the person outside who is your problem. That's not possible. And when you do the turnarounds, you see how the opposite of a painful thought can be as true or truer. At some point you arrive at statements that sound like "I should be faithful to me," "I should understand me," and ultimately "I should love me."

This might not be news to you. Most people have been told

by friends or family or advice columnists that they should love themselves. But how do you do it? The fact that you can't seem to live the turnarounds can even become another kind of self-torture. "What's the matter with me? Why can't I love myself?" You can't force this process; you can only inquire and find out what's true.

If you haven't undone your painful thoughts, you can get into a bubble bath, light candles, recite positive affirmations, pamper yourself in every way—and once you're out of the tub, the same thoughts will come back to haunt you. It's like staging a seduction, only the one you're trying to seduce is you.

This chapter is not about seducing or fooling yourself. Just the opposite: It's about un-fooling yourself. The only obstacle to loving other people is believing what you think, and you'll come to see that that's also the only obstacle to loving yourself. To discover the beliefs that may not, after all, be true for you, you'll need to ask yourself some very private questions. What are you ashamed of? Whom do you still resent (though you believe you shouldn't)? What haven't you forgiven yourself for?

This inquiry isn't manipulation. It's going inside yourself for the love of truth and finding your own answers. If you have any trouble with loving yourself, your work isn't done.

No one who thinks "I should love myself" knows what love is. Love is what we are already. So to think that you should love yourself when you don't is pure delusion. Isn't the turnaround truer? "I shouldn't love myself." How do you know that you shouldn't love yourself? You don't! That's it, for now. The truth is no respecter of spiritual concepts. "I should love myself"—ugh, on what planet? Love is not a doing. There is nothing you have to do. And when you question your mind, you can see that the only thing that keeps you from being love is a stressful thought.

Obstacles to Loving Yourself

THE THING YOU'RE MOST ASHAMED OF

A good place to start is with whatever it is you're most ashamed of. This may take some time to uncover. We're so secretive about what makes us feel ashamed that we even try to keep it from ourselves, clinging to our pretense of self-respect while our thoughts run on about how terrible we are and how unforgivable the things we've done. Secrets cry out for inquiry. You can't be free if you're hiding. And in the end, the things we're ashamed of turn out to be the greatest gifts we have to give.

We respect people who honestly let us know what they have survived and how they actually did it. When we meet someone who has come through great difficulties with an open heart, we are drawn to the truth in them, and they help us find our own truth.

I would like to show you that it's safe to see exactly what it is that you survived and to end your own denial—if only to discover the incredible gift that you have to pass on to others. I once had secrets, especially from myself, and the things I found within myself are the gifts I now share. I can go anywhere without the fear of being discovered. I can join anyone in their painful belief, because I have gone to the depths of my own painful beliefs. I have questioned them and seen them vanish like dreams. I have looked the monster straight in the eyes and seen only a child asking for my love. What else do I have of value but my own dear life? Once upon a time I was crazed with suffering. If I could do this exercise, so can you.

Exercise: "Most Ashamed"

Walk through these steps slowly. Beginning this exercise can be hard. Remember that no one but you ever needs to see what you write. This is for you, so be as honest and as fearless as you can be. You're about to step into another level of freedom.

STEP ONE.

Write down a short, simple sentence that begins "What I'm most ashamed of is _____." Example: "What I'm most ashamed of is that I deserted my children."

STEP TWO.

Write down what you think this means. Example: "I deserted my children, *and that means that* I am a terrible mother. That they'll never forgive me. That if people found out, they would be horrified and would never want to associate with me. That my children will make terrible parents and will be scarred forever." Make your own list.

STEP THREE.

Inquire into each of the "meanings" on your list, one by one. Example: "I am a terrible mother." Ask yourself: "Is it true? Can I absolutely know that it's true? How do I react when I believe that thought? Who would I be without the thought?" Then turn it around.

Once you have thoroughly inquired into this first "meaning," continue through your list. "They will never forgive me"— is it true? And so on.

Ask yourself for your own truth. Please treat each question as a deep meditation. Ask the question, then gently wait for the heart's answer to surface.

Take your time. Don't think that you know the answer yet, even if you have considered this thought hundreds of times before. The answer you have believed for years may not be the one that is true for you right now, and today's answer may surprise or even shock you. Find the answer that is true for you—no matter what it is, and even if you believe that people would condemn you for it.

Even if the turnarounds seem difficult, find three genuine ways, however modest, in which the opposite is as true as or truer than your original statement: "I am *not* a terrible mother, because I took care of them when they were sick, I made sure that they always had food, and I remembered their birthdays."

When you question your darkest secret, and turn it around, you discover that everything you thought it meant isn't necessarily true. This journey allows the mind to give you other truths, truths that reveal your goodness. There's nothing you need to hide from yourself. It's the truth that sets you free.

Another Shame Exercise: "What I Don't Want You to Know About Me"

Most of us have long mental lists of all the things we think we don't want people to know about us. What if you questioned those thoughts?

STEP ONE.

Make a list of what you think you don't want a particular person (your wife, your mother, your children), or even all of humanity, to know about you.

Here's an example of one woman's list:

What I don't want you to know about me is: My honest age is 45, my honest weight is 160, I've had two abortions, I lied when I said I cared about you, I actually married you for security, I have had three affairs that you don't know about, I never loved you with all my heart, I almost always fake my orgasms, I cheat on my taxes and lie about it, I don't think that trees are pretty and get anxious when everyone else says how beautiful they are, I often don't like anyone and pretend that I do because I think that if I'm honest people will see me as a terrible human being, I eat cookies when you're not looking and I lie about it, I hide food from you, I sometimes vomit after eating large meals, I drive too fast, I think that voting in this country is a waste of time, I think that rich people and the big corporations control every-thing anyway, whichever party wins.

STEP TWO.

Turn it around. Read your list again, but begin it with "What I *do* want you to know about me is . . ." (You don't have to tell this to the person you're thinking of. But experience it yourself. Dis-cover if any of it is as true as or truer than your original list. If possible, read your list to someone out loud, without defense or justification.)

Here's what the woman in our example wrote:

What I *do* want you to know about me is: My honest age is 45, my honest weight is 160, I've had two abortions, I lied when I said I cared about you, I actually married you for security, I have had three affairs that you don't know about, I never loved you with all my heart, I almost always fake my orgasms, I cheat on my taxes and lie about it, I don't think that trees are pretty and get anxious when everyone else says how beautiful they are, I often don't like anyone and pretend that I do because I think that if I'm honest people will see me as a terrible human being, I eat cookies when you're not looking and I lie about it, I hide food from you, I sometimes vomit after eating large meals, I drive too fast, I think that voting in this country is a waste of time, I think that rich people and the big corporations control everything anyway, whichever party wins.

I am reality: this means that I am the perfect one to be me and no one else can be it. I must be this height to be me, exactly this height, and I must be sixty-two years old. I must weigh to the ounce what I weigh, be this gender, and have my fingers on my computer keyboard in exactly this way right now. That is the requirement to be me, I notice. And there are no mistakes in this perfect world, which is a tapestry of pure delight and beauty when seen through the eyes of someone who isn't arguing with what is.

There are two ways of being me: One is to hate it and one is to love it. Which will it be (since I don't have a choice but to be me)? Okay, I'll be me, and question my thoughts about me until I see me as perfect in every way, even sweeter than perfect. Someone has got to be happy in this world. Good that it's me. I definitely volunteer.

Exercise: Letter of Apology

When we don't forgive others, we can't forgive ourselves. This won't be obvious until it is. Try the following exercise:

STEP ONE.

Think of someone who hurt you very deeply. Write that person a letter in which you do the following things. (Don't write this letter to yourself.)

Think of three things that *you* did to hurt him [or her]. Apologize. Ask him what you can do to make it right with him. Then tell him three things he gave you that you're grateful for, and thank him. Close the letter with "I love you"—if this feels right to you—and sign your name.

Here is a letter written by Sarah, a woman attending one of my two-day intensives, whose three children once refused to have anything to do with her for five years after her divorce. Those five years were the most painful of her life.

> Dearest Tony, Donna, and Dale,
>
> I am so sorry that I talked about your father to you the way I did during those terrible years of divorce. I am so sorry that I punished you for saying kind things about him. I could have learned a lot from you. I apologize for being so closed-minded, for not listening to you, and for being so harsh to you. I apologize for fighting brutally with your father in front of you and for yelling at you when you cried and asked me to stop fighting. Please tell me if there's anything I can do to make this right with you now. I'll do whatever I can.
>
> I have learned so much from each of you about unconditional love. No matter how unlovingly I have treated you, you still love me, nurture me, care for me, and always meet me with open hearts. I have learned from you the dearest ways of being

with my grandchildren just by watching you act as good parents, and good aunts and uncles, to your own and each other's children. You have taught me tenderness and courage. You always give me permission to "go for it," and you support me as I do. Thank you, children. Because of you, I can love, and I love you and others, including your father, more than I ever imagined that I was capable of. I am so grateful.

I love you,

Mom

STEP TWO.

You don't have to mail this letter. Some of us prefer to express our feelings face-to-face, telling the recipient what we have discovered, without actually reading the letter. Others of us ask the addressee for permission to read the letter, and we read it without deviating from what is written, and then listen without defense. Others never send it or make amends. Whatever you do, or don't do, you have the rest of your life to decide.

I suggest that when you're ready, you act on it as soon as possible. Act on it when you know that no matter what the response will be, you want to do it for your own sake. You do it knowing that the response is none of your business, that this letter is about your life, not the other person's. It's your life that you're cleaning up. You can't be in too big a hurry to do that.

STEP THREE.

Now turn the letter around as though you had written it to yourself. You may know the relief of forgiving another human being—how wonderful it is to love someone you thought was your enemy. Turning this letter around is also about discovery and forgiveness: of yourself. Be patient as you turn around what you have written, and discover your innocent, dear, misunderstood self. Gently move past the places where the turnaround doesn't work, and see where it does work. Take in this letter to yourself, and see how what you have written is true.

Here's how Sarah turned around the letter to her children. In it the word *you* refers to Sarah herself.

> My dearest *self*,
>
> I am so sorry that I talked about your *husband* to you the way that I did during those terrible years of divorce. I am so sorry that I punished you for *thinking* kind things about him. I could have learned a lot from you. I apologize for being so closed-minded, for not listening to you, and for being so harsh to you. I apologize for fighting brutally with your *husband* in front of you and for yelling at you when you cried and asked *yourself* to stop fighting. *You* have learned so much from *yourself* about unconditional love. No matter how unlovingly *you* have treated *yourself*, you still love *you*, nurture *you*, care for *you*, and always meet *you* with an open heart. I have learned from you the dearest ways of being with *your* grandchildren by just watching you act as a good parent to your children. You have taught me tenderness and courage. You always give *yourself* permission to "go for it," and you support *yourself* as *you* do. Thank you, *dear self*. Because of you, *you* can love, and *you* love you and others, including your *husband*, more than *you* ever imagined that *you were* capable of. I am so grateful.
>
> I love you,
> *Sarah*

You think they think there's something wrong with you. You think that other people think there's something wrong with you because *you* think it. So by gaining their approval, you've been trying to stop them from thinking what you are thinking. The worst that can happen is that they are just like you! It's their job to think what you're already thinking, until you question it. When you question what you think, the truth will make you laugh. And when you laugh, they laugh too. Everybody does their job all the time. That's why meeting your thought system is so much fun.

MAKING FRIENDS WITH CRITICISM

If you really want to be free, criticism from others can be a gift. Feeling hurt by any criticism, feeling the slightest urge to defend yourself, means that there's something you don't accept and love about yourself. This is the very part of you that you want to hide. You want to be loved and understood, but not there. And as we've seen, hiding creates separation, from yourself as well as from others.

What's the worst thing anyone could say about you? That you are very aggressive? *Are* you sometimes? Well then, they're right! So the worst thing that could happen is that they'd tell you the truth. Isn't that what you want? When someone says, "You're aggressive!" you could say, "You know, I can see it that way too." And there's peace. Or you could say, "No, I'm not! You're the aggressive one!"—and you know where that leads.

No matter what anyone says to or about you, if you experience stress, then you are the one who's suffering in the moment. Stress is the signal that it's time to question your own thinking. Once you understand how to hear criticism and experience the value of it, you may want to give yourself the gift of the following exercise.

Exercise: Criticism

STEP ONE.

When someone criticizes you and says you are wrong, unkind, unclear, uncaring, feel it. Settle into it. Ask yourself, "Is it true? Could she be right? Can I see how someone might see me that way?" Wait for the answer. See if you can respond only with

"Thank you for letting me know that. You could be right." (You can say this to her silently or in actual words.) How does this feel?

STEP TWO.

After the criticism, ask yourself, "Was hearing that remark at all stressful?" If the answer is yes, it means that the criticism is true for you, and you haven't dealt with it or gone deep enough yet to understand your own pain. See what happens when you question the thoughts that put you on the defensive.

Example: Maybe you were hurt when your friend said, "You don't listen to me." The thought that hurt you might be, "She's wrong about me." Is it true that she's wrong? (She's telling you what she thinks. She has to be right about that.) Now question the thought.

> *"She's wrong about me"*—*is it true?* No, it's not. The truth is that sometimes I don't listen.
>
> *How do I react when I believe that she's wrong?* I immediately get upset and feel unjustly accused. I start defending myself. I attack her in my mind. I feel sorry for myself. I stop listening.
>
> *Who would I be without the thought "She's wrong about me"?* I might listen. I might be open to what she's saying. This is scary. I might take a deeper look at myself.
>
> *Turn it around:* "I'm wrong about her when I think she's wrong about me."

When you no longer put your energy into seeking approval, you can open your arms to criticism and see it as a gift, instead of as something to disprove or defend against. Being honest and vulnerable ends the illusion of being manipulated or discovered in any way. When you're genuinely humble, there's no way that criticism can hurt you; it becomes obvious, through your own experience, that it can only help you. This is how clarity takes on life as effective action, so that you are kind to others and kind to yourself.

Defense is the first act of war. If you tell me that I'm mean, rejecting, hard, unkind, unfair, I say, "Thank you, sweetheart, I can find all these in my life, I have been everything you say, and more. Tell me everything you see, and together we can help me understand. Through you, I come to know myself. Without you, how can I know the places in me that are unkind and invisible? You bring me to myself. So, sweetheart, look into my eyes and tell me again. I want you to give me everything." This is how friends meet. It's called integrity. I am all things. If you see me as unkind, that is an opportunity for me to go inside and look at what appears in my life. Have I ever been unkind? I can find it. Have I ever acted unfairly? That doesn't take me long to acknowledge. If I'm a bit cloudy about it, my children can fill me in. What could anyone call me that I couldn't find at some time in my life? If you say one single thing that I have the urge to defend, that thing is the very pearl waiting inside me to be discovered.

11

LIVING IN LOVE

⚮

When you start to find genuine love, the ways you used to manipulate people to get what you thought was love suddenly become clear and obvious. You might expect this to be embarrassing; in fact, it's often funny, and you find that it's easy to forgive yourself for your own humanity. You realize that the old ways of seeking approval were just a misunderstanding that has been cleared up now, and you are grateful for that.

I sent out an e-mail asking how inquiry had worked for people. The replies kept coming in, five hundred pages of them. As I read, I was moved by how much people had suffered, in so many different ways, and by the delight they took in waking up from the dream of what they thought was happening in their lives and seeing what was really happening. Inquiry seemed like a magic realm that they could come home to after a long, amazing journey, a house where they could sit around the fire, telling tales of danger overcome, and laughing with old friends. When you don't believe your stressful thoughts, all that's left are love and laughter.

This chapter is taken from just a few of those responses.

No Kissing

I pursued Lena for four years to no effect. I fixed her computer, I ate onion rings because she liked them, I pulled out my funniest remarks, I underplayed how much I wanted her. Nothing worked.

Then she and I had a chance to spend a weekend together. She made it clear that *no* form of sexual contact was okay. I wasn't allowed to hold her hand, to hug her, to give her a kiss on the cheek—nothing. Every time the urge to show affection arose, I had to not act. Instead, I noticed my thoughts. And this is what I saw: that I used all those techniques to make women like me. All that weekend, instead of feeling like I was repressing myself, I noticed that those simple physical actions actually dissipated the loving, fun, sexy sensations I was feeling. Without the usual outlet, those feelings just kept running through my body. At the end of this totally platonic weekend, I had never been more blissed out and full of love!

The key moment when I stopped seeking her love was, to say the least, a huge relief. My whole body relaxed. I simply couldn't make myself believe that I needed a relationship with her, or with anyone else, to be happy. I stopped feeling pulled outside myself, I stopped reaching for happiness where it didn't and couldn't exist. I just stopped doing what I had been doing my whole life. As a result, I felt stable and honest and complete for the first time.

I stopped seeking this woman's love, and I apologized for all the ways I tried to get her to agree with my thought that we should be a couple. I genuinely—and I was shocked by this—had no desire to be with her in a committed relationship, and I felt content with the fact that I loved a woman who didn't want to be with me that way. Well, the great ironic punch line to the story is that the moment I stopped seeking her love and approval, when I could no longer find a *reason* to be with her (or anyone else, for that matter), she looked at me and thought, "The freedom that I've always wanted—I can find it with Steven. Oh, and he's pretty cute!" And she leaned over and kissed me.

Now, four years later, we've been married for a year. And our actual relationship is much better than the one I was imagining for all those years.

Cooking for Love

I used to believe that if I fed people I was giving them love, and in return they would give love back to me. When I realized I was doing that, I was in shock. I didn't know what to do with myself. What did I have to give if I couldn't cook for people?

I was startled, confused, and dismayed when it started dawning on me that I was a slave, that my life was all about pleasing others. I felt that I had lost something very precious. I cried a lot. Who is this girl that I am? What does she want? I didn't know. I was clueless.

I knew I had to love myself in order to be able to see love out there. But how do I *do* that? I kept on doggedly questioning and turning around the thoughts that came up in me. The more I investigated them, the less interested I was in getting other people's approval. I realized that what was important was getting my own approval.

When I cook for someone now, I'm genuinely interested in whether they like it, but I don't depend on their approval. I don't wait with bated breath to see if they are pleased, and I'm not crushed if they aren't enthusiastic. If someone criticizes a meal, instead of being hurt and resisting or dismissing their comments, I consider the possibility that they are right, and their comments often turn out to be helpful. When a meal is okay but didn't turn out as well as I had planned, I serve it without fuss or apology and just enjoy the company. I never would have been able to do that in the past. This brings me peace and space and the ability to be present with whatever happens.

Toaster Oven

I used to live only to please others; now I do things that I really want to do, not the things I think I should do. For example, I let a church member stay at my house until she found another place. Then, one evening, I found her asleep, drunk, with a frozen dinner in the toaster oven. I realized I didn't trust her not to burn my house down. So I told her she had to leave. In the past, I would have lived with the fear and hoped she would find a place soon. This time, I just told her what I was afraid of. She quickly found another place she likes and thanked me for being so clear and respectful with her.

Capricious Woman

I was living alone and seeing a woman who tended to cancel our dates at the last moment, leaving me forlorn and sorry for myself, like Charlie Chaplin in *The Gold Rush*. I would tell her it didn't matter and that I was fine on my own. I wasn't, but I thought she'd drop me completely if I seemed needy. I followed the instructions for inquiry, judged her furiously, wrote it down, asked four questions, turned it around, had realizations, and still felt miserable when she didn't want to see me. Then one Saturday evening, as I was approaching my empty house, I felt a slight thrill as if I were about to meet someone interesting. I was bewildered for a moment. Had I forgotten about a houseguest? Then it came to me: the interesting person I was about to meet inside my house was the one walking toward it. It seemed like a small thing at the time, but that forlorn feeling never came back. Also, that capricious girlfriend stopped canceling our dates and is now my capricious wife.

A Visit to an Old Friend

I had been questioning my mind intensely for some time— mostly on my ex-wife. The revelations kept coming even when I wasn't consciously doing inquiry. One day I went to have lunch with a dear friend of mine whom I hadn't seen for seven or eight months. I respect this man very much and always enjoy seeing him. But this visit was different. Speaking with him was a completely new experience, and I felt closer to him than ever before. I noticed that he wasn't doing anything different from what he usually did. The change was in me, and the thoughts were undoing them- selves. For example, I noticed that when I told him about a recent achievement of mine, which I was very proud of, I didn't care whether or not he appreciated how great a job I had done. The phone rang in the middle of the conversation, and he picked it up, and I noticed that I didn't take the interruption personally. In fact, I felt a wave of affection for my friend as he talked to a business colleague of his; I understood that he is a man who thinks he needs to answer the phone every time it rings.

As I listened to myself talk to him, I was vividly aware of the difference between now and the last conversation we'd had. Then, it was as if I had been sitting on the edge of my seat, leaning toward him, constantly looking for his approval. When he had seemed uninterested in what I was saying, I had felt hurt and had backed away from him; when he had answered the phone, I had felt ever so mildly insulted. And now, all this was gone. I realized that I didn't need a thing from him, that it didn't matter in the least whether or not he was interested in my words. *I* was interested; *I* approved; *I* was delighted with myself. Actually, I spent much of the time just listening to my friend. Some of what he said was fascinating, some of it was less so, but during the whole conversation I was filled with love for him, and that was all that was important. And I hadn't even done The Work on him!

A Great Story While It Lasted

Five years ago, within two weeks, my father committed suicide, I lost my job, and my partner left me to be with a woman who had just moved next door. He and his new lover were constant reminders of what had happened to me; it was like Chinese water torture. I could see them in the driveway, pulling in and out, working on the lawn, mowing her lawn instead of mine, sitting on the porch as I would come and go from the house. I even thought I could feel them in their bedroom next to my kitchen, a distance of about twenty feet.

I begged him to come back. I threatened him with karmic retribution for leaving me. I begged the other woman to send him home. I begged his mother to plead with him to come home to me. I sent my kids over to plead. I literally fell on my knees in their driveway and begged him not to leave me all alone at a time like this. I was such a martyr! I wanted him to come back to me, and then spend however long it took making it up to me. I wanted him to suffer the way I did.

Well, he didn't, he didn't want to oblige me, he was in love and having fun. It wasn't until I wrote out a Worksheet that I saw that by trying to punish him, I was really punishing me! Not only me, but my kids too. If I had just let him go to do what he needed to do, I could have gotten on with my life, rather than trying to make him feel bad (and why would someone want to come back to a person who tries to make him feel bad?). "He should come back to me"—is it true? I don't think so. How do I react when I believe that? Rage, misery, nastiness, manipulation. The turnarounds were amazing, especially "I should come back to myself." That one hit me like lightning. I had a whole life to come back to, and my kids as well. Once I really got this, I began to heal from the pain of the breakup. I didn't spend so much of my kids' early childhood grieving over him. I played with them more and spent more time reading books to them and telling them stories.

My ex had to make his own choices and do what his heart told him to do, not what my agenda told him. Inquiry showed me that he was responsible for his happiness, and I was responsible for mine. All the self-righteous suffering in the world couldn't change that. The suffering stopped the day I began to seriously question my thoughts. I finally understood that it was my own thinking that was making me miserable, not my ex-partner. I quit trying to torture and manipulate. I quit trying to win everyone else's sympathy by showing them how pathetic I was. Instead, I finally understood that he left me once, but I left myself a thousand times, every single day for the next four years.

Inquiry set me free, and let me clear my mind to the point where now I can laugh at myself and be happy for him. It was a great story while it lasted, but boy, have I felt better since I dropped it!

Because I Am

I used to threaten to leave; now I realize this is none of my business. I see that as long as I am with him, I need to be with him—that only when I actually leave him do I need to leave. And so far, I haven't. This is so cool! It's one of the best things that ever happened to me after I began to question my thoughts. It gives me so much freedom. No more worries about "What am I doing here? What's wrong with me?" I am living with him because I am. Period. In the hardest times, when my thoughts multiply like crazy, at least I can count on that. This is an island of peace, solid ground that I can stand on.

Angry Colleague

At work I have a colleague who's often angry. She has never failed to trigger a defensive reaction in me. But this week when she came to me with an angry complaint, I remained completely settled in myself. I knew that her anger had nothing to do with me and was able to treat her with love.

When I told her she was right to complain, her anger dissolved, and she gave me a wry smile, as if *she* were a naughty child who'd been found out.

Falling in Love with My Mother

I resented my mother for being so ill for so long. I resented the burden she was for my dad and me. I used to suffer because I thought she was so ungrateful to those of us who sacrificed our lives to take care of her. After questioning my painful thoughts about her for several months, I realized that I was a fraud! I wasn't acting out of love toward her, I was getting attention for being the "suffering good daughter"! I was making up this *grand* story so that people would sympathize with me, and all the time I could barely stand to hear my mother's voice on the phone. Once I caught on to my delusions, I was able to see this perfectly beautiful woman who had been ill most of her life, and who was strong and independent and full of love. I fell in love with my mom. I was eager to sit with her and do whatever was needed. I sat with her in this state of love for three days while she was dying. I am so happy I was able to love my mom while she was still here.

My Wild Affair

I wanted wild encounters with my lover, to be touched, to be more sexually stimulated than I was with my husband, to bring adventure back into my life by transgressing the social rules. I wanted him to see me as adventurous, sexually attractive, young and beautiful (I'm in my late 30s), intelligent, articulate, and desirable in every way. I tried to be perfect, to respond to his (mostly sexual) needs, to be always ready for him, able to handle any situation without being emotional. I created a veil of deceit around my husband to hide the betrayal. Pretending to meet every one of my lover's needs was the way I dealt with my fear of being rejected. Being exactly how he expected me to be was the only way I knew to win his heart. As it turned out, this had an unexpected kind of magnetic repulsion. I didn't win his heart. It actually drove him away.

I didn't like myself during that process; it kept me a victim of my own expectations. Betraying my husband was a form of my own lack of trust and safety within. I also betrayed myself by keeping my self-esteem really low. I felt guilty all the time. I was constantly stepping past my own boundaries and punishing myself for doing that. I was just not living in the present moment; I always wanted things to be different. I wanted my husband to be wilder and sexier, like my lover, and I wanted my lover to be steady and dependable, like my husband.

Just by noticing how desperately I was seeking love and approval, my life started to change in a huge way. I suddenly had more love than I could handle. After my lover ended the affair, I realized that I can only ultimately belong to myself. My relationships improved on all levels.

I had always resented my husband for being self-centered; now if such a thought enters my mind, I question it. I like it when I judge him without censoring myself, like an angry child, and then investigate each of my thoughts and turn them around. I like letting him be who he is, without wanting to change him. It's so much easier now to say no to him and feel good about it.

I know now that love comes from inside me. Every moment is precious as it is, and my angry or hurt thoughts teach me how to look even deeper within. For example, I used to think that I needed my husband not to travel as much as he does; now I enjoy it when he is here and when he isn't here. What he does is his own business, and it rarely affects the happiness in my heart.

Now I can be insulted, blamed, spat at, sworn at (I'm bringing up teenagers), and my inner peace is stable. I can stay calm and loving as long as I question my stressful thoughts.

The House Gets Cleaned or Not

My husband doesn't enjoy cleaning the house, and when I used to get fed up with him, I would think that I'd have to end our marriage and find someone else who would honor me and support me better. Now I am more committed to my marriage then ever before. The house gets cleaned or not. I realized that it doesn't have to be perfectly clean at all times. It never was perfect anyway. Before, it wasn't perfect and we had lots of arguments; now, it isn't perfect and I have peace.

A Turnaround

I read *Loving What Is* within the space of a weekend, hardly stopping to eat. On Sunday I began to feel that my wife and children were being suspiciously considerate to me, as if it were my birthday. Finally I asked my wife, "What's going on here? What are you planning? Why are you all being so nice to me?"

My wife stared at me and started laughing. "We're not doing anything different," she said. "You're the one who has changed; you're the one who's acting kinder!"

Toilet Bowl Gratitude

We used to fight over chores. I got really upset that I was always the one cleaning the house, doing the dishes and the laundry, cleaning the bathroom and the toilet, even though I was the only one with a full-time job. This drove me nuts. Soon after beginning to do inquiry as a regular practice, I was cleaning the toilet bowl and suddenly I felt enormously grateful for life. Cleaning the bowl meant that I was a wonderful mother providing food for my daughters and I was cleaning up the food after its transformation in their beautiful bodies. I didn't care anymore who was cleaning or who wasn't. I was just following directions, from inside me. After that episode, more and more family members showed interest in cleaning the bathroom. It was amazing.

A Living Saint

I like to attend church. I've always wanted the people in church to see me not just as spiritual but as someone like Jesus or Mother Teresa. I don't want people just to think I'm good, I want them to see me with rays of golden light streaming out from me like the angels on *Touched by an Angel*, and I want everyone to bask in my wonderfulness and be a little envious that they haven't attained it yet. I know this sounds ridiculous, but I have devoted years of my life to activities that I seriously believed would make me appear this way.

Then I taught a weekly class in a women's prison. I never took the time to really listen to these women or discover what they were feeling, because I was so intent on teaching them and having them see me as a great and holy teacher. One night a woman threw herself on the floor and started screaming that she had killed her baby. She screamed in agony for hours. It suddenly occurred to me that I hadn't been listening or connecting with these women at all, that my interest was in how they were seeing me. Perhaps they needed forgiveness. They wanted someone to show them that they were okay and their lives could go on, regardless of what they had done. No, it was the other way around: *I* needed forgiveness. I wanted *them* to show *me* that I was okay and that my life could go on, regardless of what *I* had done. And I saw it.

I was deeply shocked at my own arrogance. I was disappointed with myself, suddenly aware that I had been fooling myself all these years. The shock made me begin to question the thoughts that had led me into such dishonesty. I was really serious about finding my own truth. I wrote dozens of Worksheets every day, many of them on how angry I was at God for all the misery in the world and in my own life.

I stopped every volunteer activity that I did when there was an audience, though I still do volunteer work one-on-one. I spared myself and others the pain of my performances. I stopped trying to be Jesus, and the more I questioned my thoughts, the more content I became with being myself. I stopped blaming God for my own misery and started truly taking responsibility for my own life.

I feel much more peaceful now. It's wonderful to know there's nothing I have to do to prove my value to others. I started seeing what's good about myself and not trying to manufacture a holiness that would win admiration and approval from others. Most people like to be around me now, because I enjoy laughing and that makes them laugh. I may never be a saint, but I don't need to be a saint. I'm a much happier, kinder person today. I'm really starting to like myself.

Rules

I had a lot of rules. I had a rule about being kissed goodbye
if he was going somewhere. If he didn't kiss me, I'd call him
back and make him kiss me. I had a rule about having sex. If
he wanted to, I would never refuse. If I wanted to, he was
allowed to refuse, but I would feel resentful. I had a rule
about him being loving and nice to my children and if he
wasn't, I'd either have a fight with him or withdraw completely. I had a rule about him being responsible for certain
"man" things such as pouring the wine, changing plugs, getting the barbecue ready, and I was irritable if he left me to
do these things. Also, he loves cooking, and because he
didn't cook the way I do, I used to argue him out of doing it
so that it could be done my way.

That has all changed since I began to do inquiry as a
regular practice. I allow him to kiss me if that's what he
wants to do, and it's fine if he doesn't. I will ask him for sex
if it's what I want, and I don't get hurt or resentful if he says
no. If he wants sex and I don't, I feel comfortable saying no.
I love my children, and he doesn't have to. It's his business,
and if he doesn't spend time with them, it's okay with me
(of course, I love it when he does spend time with them).
He pours the wine if he offers to, otherwise I do it. The
same applies to changing plugs or preparing a barbecue.
And now I just enjoy his cooking.

I'm beginning to understand that love doesn't go anywhere—it never *isn't*. I can't always embrace this understanding, but it's something that I experience more and more. I still
have thoughts that say "I need your love," and then, right
away, I find myself thinking, "Is that true?" and I smile.

Dancing with My Teddy Bear

One evening, after about a month when my partner didn't want any sex with me and I was miserable and hurt about it, I questioned my thoughts, thoughts such as "I need him to find me desirable" and "We should be having sex." Soon I found that I was just enjoying myself, needing no sex after all, not even from me, dancing with my teddy bear, in my pajamas and socks, with no makeup, moved by a beautiful song about love and gratitude. I was so happy with myself. He came back home and just looked at me. After so many weeks of trying to convince him to have sex with me, he dragged me to the bedroom for a very sweet time together, with wonderful sex.

What I love about that is the peace of just being happy to see him come home. I enjoyed the simplicity of it. I enjoyed not trying to be sexy or to present myself a certain way to turn him on. I enjoyed being with myself with my teddy bear. And I enjoyed being with my man.

I am still working on the thought that I can manipulate him to have sex with me by being happy with myself! I can see that it's not true. When I'm truly happy with myself, I really don't need anything else, and I can't control whether that will turn him on or not.

We Used to Fight

We used to fight. Now, when she is angry at me, she fills out a Judge-Your-Neighbor Worksheet [page 251] and reads all her complaints to me. I know that if I can't hear her judgments, find ways in which every one of them is true, and tell her how and where she's right (she usually doesn't know the half of it!), then *I'm* the one with the problem, regardless of what I think she's doing. And I know that if I do hear her and find the truth of what she's saying (she's never been wrong yet), whatever seemed to be the problem disappears. In fact, once I do that, genuinely and not as some technique, the next thing she'll often say is, "And here's how *I* do that same thing I was just accusing you of."

My wife used to be afraid of telling me things that were upsetting. Now she knows she can tell me anything, and the eventual result (sometimes it's immediate, sometimes it takes me a few hours) is that we become closer.

I used to complain (only in my mind) about things I wanted her to do, especially sexually, and then resent her, snap at her, pick fights with her, and make both of us unhappy. I wouldn't tell her these things because I was afraid she would get upset to hear that our marriage wasn't living up to my expectations.

Now I know that I don't need the things I want. I can bring them up as a conversation instead of a demand. And this allows me to listen to her and actually hear and understand her, instead of seeing her reasons as the cause of my problems. And if she does react and get upset by the conversation, I don't feel the need to run away or try to make her feel better.

I used to think sex was a way of making someone accept and like me because of what I could do for them. Now, it's more of a conversation, more of a way of exploring other aspects of my relationship beyond "who can do what for whom" (though that's sometimes part of the game too).

God's Counselor

As a result of doing inquiry, the most stunning improvement is in my relationship with myself. I love my own company. I laugh a lot and sometimes just cry from the beauty of it all. Sometimes I get wrapped up in a stressful belief and then I just dissolve in laughter. I love the humility I feel when I realize how important I thought I was, when I wasn't important at all. I used to confuse my business and God's business. It's a relief to give up being God's counselor. Life just seems to flow through me now. I notice what I'm doing, and then I notice the next thing. I don't seem to plan much, but it all gets done.

Looking for Approval by Giving Advice

I used to give all my friends advice about how they should live, and I felt angry because I spent so much time and energy doing this and no one listened to me or was there for my own problems. I think that's hilarious now, because I see that I wasn't there for myself. Some of my friendships disappeared when I questioned my thinking and stopped managing them. Other friendships are much deeper than they were.

You're So Negative

I used to hate my husband's negativity; now I embrace it because it shows me where *I* have some negativity about something within me. I realize that if I didn't believe my thoughts about my husband's negativity, I wouldn't be upset.

When he criticizes me now, I don't shut down. I actually listen to what he has to say, and I can find where it's true. I'm getting to know a pretty amazing man—after nine years of being with him.

Standing at the Ferry Terminal

My example of inquiry is pretty simple, but it helped me remove a block in my relationships with other people that has been around for over thirty years. I'm a working husband and support my wife and extended family. Every day my wife drops me at the ferry and picks me up in the evening when I come back from the city. Some evenings she is late, and a few times, particularly when she was working for a dance company, she was very late or completely forgot me, because she was engrossed in what she was doing.

I hated it when that happened. I felt like she didn't love me, didn't appreciate the shit I deal with on a daily basis to support the family, while she works at what she loves doing. She doesn't get well paid for it either, so now I am supporting the dance company as well. I would call her to find out where she was, she'd realize she had forgotten me, she'd apologize, I'd get furious with her, because I felt her part-time, low-level, practically unpaid work was more important to her than I was.

Then I discovered The Work.

One day I asked myself: "Is it true that because she's late she doesn't love me?" I couldn't say that it was true. I asked myself, "Can I absolutely know whether it's true that she doesn't love me because she doesn't remember to pick me up on time?" I can't know that. I asked myself, "Who

would I be without the thought that she doesn't love me?"
I'd be a much happier person. Duh!

I realized, and realize daily, that she does love me. I realized that it was my *thoughts* about being left behind, when
everyone else from the ferry was being picked up or walking
home, that were making me angry and upset. Without these
thoughts I didn't have a problem. I explained this to my
wife, and she just laughed at me, but said if it worked, then
she was happy. And it did work, and I didn't feel like swear-
ing at her at the end of the day.

I didn't take inquiry on this issue any further at the time.

Several months later, my brother came to stay with us.
One day we were talking about things, and I told him how I
used to get upset when my wife was late, and about the realization I'd had. He asked me if I remembered what happened to us as children, and I couldn't remember. It turns out
that my mother and father both used to forget to pick us up
from school, and the same thing happened later when we
had our first jobs as fledgling adults. I had blocked this from
my mind, but when he reminded me, the memories flooded
back. I used to feel awful at being the last kid to be picked
up or at having to walk home. Often the excuse was "I was
busy at work" (my parents had their own business). Sometimes there was no excuse, not even an apology.

As soon as I remembered this, my other revelation hit
me with renewed force, about my wife loving me, and not
being uncaring when she failed to pick me up. The
thoughts that had made me angry were just thoughts—
they had nothing to do with my wife.

That was the beginning of my use of inquiry on a daily
basis. It makes me saner, and more likely to accept the stuff
that happens, rather than make it personal. It's not a great
spiritual awakening, and I am not a saint unruffled by daily

life. But I have an amazing tool now that I can use in any stressful situation. I still get upset, but I never have to *stay* upset ever again.

Off the Pedestal

I wanted Tom to be my best friend forever and never leave me for another woman. I wanted lots of sex, attention, gifts, his pledge of eternal love, and his recognition that I was his soul mate. I grew my hair for him, because he thought long hair was a turn-on. I lost thirty pounds because he liked me slimmer. I even studied scripture because he was really into that. I did whatever I could to please him. I never said no, because I believed that love never says no. (I can hardly believe this now! But that's what I thought.)

I told him I was happy when I really wasn't.

I loved being on Tom's pedestal for a while. I loved that he saw me as wise, good, and beautiful. He asked me for advice every day, and that made me feel powerful. When his approval began to slip, I did whatever I thought it would take to win it back. It was an endless, exhausting cycle.

Around this time a girlfriend told me about The Work, and we'd do it together. It took me a while to find the thought that was dragging me down, even though—or maybe because—my whole life turned around it. Then I found it: *I need Tom's approval,* and I asked the questions.

Now, I see that while I still love Tom I don't *need* him anymore. And I certainly don't need his approval. I have my own. For the first time I just say what I want and what I don't want in the moment. This usually means that I don't listen to him read scripture (although I do read it on my own when I feel like it). And I've cut my hair very short.

Funnily enough, Tom likes it better that way: he says I'm very sexy, and I tease him for thinking I should have it long. We're both having so much more fun now.

Ex-boyfriend

My ex-boyfriend came around a couple of weeks ago. This is usually awful for me. He's a beautiful man, in my opinion, just gorgeous, and it messes me up when he comes over, because I wish he were still mine. This time, because of all the inquiry I had done, I was able to just be there with him without expecting anything. I did notice the thought "I wish he were still my boyfriend." And instantly I saw that he was still my boyfriend: after all, there he was. And what was he?

He talked and talked about himself, about how his ex-wife always did things wrong. I noticed he wasn't interested in what I had to say, he was interested in telling me what a bitch she was. It sounded a lot like the story he used to tell me several years ago. He looked so handsome, and I had the thought that I wasn't interested in what he had to say either. So I lay down on the floor and just listened to the sound of his voice, like music. I didn't encourage him or agree with his sad story, which is what I had done in the past.

He lay down by me and began to caress me. I said I didn't want to make love with him, although it seemed very interesting. He told me I was a cock-teaser. I smiled and said he could be right. As he was leaving, he hugged me, and we kissed. He said he would be calling me. In the past I would have waited for him to call, hoping it was him each time the phone rang. This time that didn't happen. I don't know what I'll do if he calls; it's not on my "radar" because it isn't happening right now. I have only loving feelings about him, because I am clear that I don't know what he should or shouldn't be doing. I truly have no idea what should or shouldn't happen. I feel gratitude for what I have, which is so much.

Forgive Me

My first experience with The Work involved an incident with my then nineteen-year-old daughter. She was resenting me for being on drugs when she was gestating. I am no longer a drug addict, and haven't been since she was three, and I very much wanted her to forgive me. I wrote a Worksheet on her, and one of my statements was "I want her to be loving toward me, no matter what happened in the past." The turnaround was "I want to be loving toward her, no matter what happens in the present." No matter how angry or hateful or resentful she acts toward me, I want to be loving toward her. That was so important to realize! It helped me acknowledge that she might never find a way to forgive me for putting her at risk when she was in my womb. And I could also acknowledge that she might always be angry at me, and that would be okay, because it would be what is.

A few months later, she realized that I had made tremendous progress recovering from my drug addiction and that I had done a pretty good job raising her, taking her from her father's drug-filled house, and turning our lives in a more healthy direction. She told me she loves me and forgives me.

Sex Partner

I used to think that the only way I could be truly happy is if I found my soul mate. I went through three marriages and three divorces because they were soooo imperfect! Through inquiry I found myself, and I also discovered that each husband *was* my perfect partner. Each of them had brought me to where I was right now.

Another thing I noticed was that I never made love before. I'd always had sex. After applying The Work in my life, I found out how to enjoy everything about lovemaking without thoughts of whether I was pleasing my partner or not, whether I was too fat or too old, and on and on. I discovered that I didn't need my partner's approval, and I began to have the best time ever. I remember this very clearly because I cried. I actually *felt* another person's body and experienced something I had been seeking during sex all my life. It was so sexy! And to think that all I had to do was question my thoughts, and let them let go of me!

Love Without Need

My partner and I were trying to arrange for me to meet a new friend of hers whom she liked very much and thought I would too. We never seemed to find a time when we could all meet at once. So I suggested that I just arrange to meet her on my own. To her dismay, my sweetheart discovered a whole bunch of fearful ideas like "They'll get to be better friends with each other than with me," "He'll leave me and go live with her." Immediately we stopped making plans and sat down to inquire into these thoughts together, and eventually she came to one realization that really mattered to her: "I don't need you." She looked right into my eyes and said that to me, and I said it back to her, because in that moment I truly found it too. It was a moment of stunning intimacy for us. I felt a vast, spacious communion, an effortless, promiseless, deal-free marriage with her, and with myself-as-her. It was like rocking in the womb, so safe. It seems now like the real basis of our relationship, both beautiful and true. When I forget it, I feel miserable, and that reminds me to look for what anxieties I'm putting between me and that place of homecoming.

I have chosen examples that show you the ordinariness of the process of freedom so you can see that anyone, in any situation, can do inquiry. Once you've noticed the very simple secret of questioning your thoughts, you'll find that either you're happily moving along in your life, feeling love, and doing what you want to do and what seems loving, or, if you hit a bump, you're inquiring into the thoughts that separate you from reality and from the experience of love. And the four questions and turnaround return you to happily moving along. Eventually The Work just becomes something very simple, a way of maintaining a happy life.

When you believe the thought
that anyone should love you,
that's where the pain begins. I
often say, "If I had a prayer, it
would be: God spare me from
the desire for love, approval, or
appreciation. Amen."

12

LOVE ITSELF

❧

Love is what you are already. Love doesn't seek anything. It's already complete. It doesn't want, doesn't need, has no *shoulds*. It already has everything it wants, it already *is* everything it wants, just the way it wants it. So when I hear people say that they love someone and want to be loved in return, I know they're not talking about love. They're talking about something else.

Sometimes you may seem to trade love for the stressful thought appearing in the moment. It's a little trip out into illusion. Seeking love is how you lose the awareness of love. But you can only lose the awareness of it, not the state. That's not an option, because love is what we all are. That's immovable. When you investigate your stressful thinking and your mind becomes clear, love pours into your life, and there's nothing you can do about it.

Love joins everything, without condition. It doesn't avoid the nightmare; it looks forward to it and then inquires. There is no way to join except to get free of your belief that you want something from your partner. That's true joining. It's like "Bingo! You just won the lottery!"

If I want something from my partner, I simply ask. If he says no and I have a problem with that, I need to take a look at my thinking. Because I already have everything. We all do. That's how I can sit here so comfortably: I don't want anything from you that you don't want to give. I don't even want your freedom if you don't. I don't even want your peace.

The truth that you experience is how I'm able to join with you. That's how you touch me, and you touch me so intimately that it brings tears to my eyes. I've joined you, and you don't have a choice. And I do this over and over and over, endlessly, effortlessly. It's called making love.

Love wouldn't deny a breath. It wouldn't deny a grain of sand or a speck of dust. It is totally in love with itself, and it delights in acknowledging itself through its own presence, in every way, without limit. It embraces it all, everything from the murderer and the rapist to the saint to the dog and cat. Love is so vast within itself that it will burn you up. It's so vast that there's nothing you can do with it. All you can do is be it.

FURTHER TOOLS
FOR INQUIRY

❧

The list below includes the four questions together with several follow-up questions that you may find useful when investigating a resistant thought.

1. Is it true?

If your answer is no, continue to question 3.
    Possible follow-ups:

- What is the reality of it? Did it happen? (This is often the first question to ask when the thought you're investigating involves a *should*—"My husband should listen to me," "This shouldn't be happening." Inquiry is concerned only with reality. "He should"—when he doesn't—is a thought that argues with reality. This is not helpful when you're inquiring into what's true. What husbands should do is what they do. So the answer to "He should care—is it true?" will always be no, until you think he does care. "This shouldn't be happening" couldn't possibly be true unless it isn't happening.)

2. Can you absolutely know that it's true?

Possible follow-ups:

- Can you know more than God/reality?
- Whose business are you in?
- Can you really know what is best in the long run for his/her/your path?
- Can you absolutely know that you would be happier, or that your life would be better, if you got what you wanted?

3. How do you react when you believe that thought?

Possible follow-ups:

- Where does the feeling hit you, where do you feel it in your body when you believe that thought? Describe it. What do your feelings reveal to you when you think that thought? Allow your feelings to live, and notice how much of your body they take over. Where do those feelings take you?

- What pictures, if any, come to you when you believe that thought?
- How do you treat others when you believe that thought? What specifically do you say to them? What specifically do you do? Whom does your mind attack and how? In describing your reaction, provide as much detail as you can.
- How do you treat yourself when you believe that thought? Is this where addictions kick in and you reach for food, alcohol, credit cards, the TV remote? Do you have thoughts of self-hatred? What are they?
- How have you lived your life when you believed that thought? Be specific. Go into your past.
- Where does your mind travel when you believe that thought?
- Whose business are you in when you believe that thought?
- Does that thought bring peace or stress into your life?
- What do you get for holding that belief?
- Can you see a reason to drop that thought (and please don't try to drop it)?
- Can you see a stress-free reason to keep that thought? If yes, make a list. Are these reasons really stress-free? How does the stress affect your life and work?

4. Who would you be without the thought?

Possible follow-ups:

- Who would you be if you didn't believe that thought?
- Close your eyes and imagine yourself with that person (or in that situation) without that thought. Describe how it feels. What do you see?

- Imagine that you are meeting this person for the very first time with no beliefs about him or her. What do you see?
- Who are you *right now*, sitting here without that thought?
- How would you live your life without that thought? If you were incapable of thinking that thought, how would your life be different?
- How would you treat others differently without that thought?

Turn the thought around

Statements can be turned around to yourself, to the other, and to the opposite. Find three examples in your life of where the turn-arounds are as true or truer. Be specific, and as detailed as you can.

Possible follow-ups:

- Is this turnaround as true as or truer than your original statement?
- Where do you experience this turnaround in your life now?
- If you lived this turnaround, what would you do, or how would you live differently?
- Do you see any other turnarounds that seem as true or truer?

THE JUDGE-YOUR-NEIGHBOR WORKSHEET

**Judge your neighbor • Write it down •
Ask four questions • Turn it around**

Fill in the blanks below, writing about someone you haven't yet forgiven one hundred percent. (**Do not write about yourself yet.**) Use short, simple sentences. Don't censor yourself—allow yourself to be critical and petty. Try to fully experience the anger or pain as if the situation were occurring right now. Take this opportunity to express your judgments on paper.

1. Who angers, frustrates, or confuses you, and why? Whom do you resent? What is it about that person that you don't like?

   (For example: I am *angry* at *Paul* because *he doesn't listen to me, he doesn't appreciate me, he argues with everything I say.*)

I am _____ at _____ because _____
                                          (Name)

_____

_____

_____

2. How do you want that person to change? What do you want that person to do?

I want _____ to _____
          (Name)

_____

_____

_____

3. What is it that the person should or shouldn't do, be, think, or feel? What advice could you offer?

_____ should/shouldn't _____
   (Name)

_____

_____

_____

4. What does that person need to do in order for you to be happy?

I need _____ to _____
           (Name)

_____

_____

_____

5. What do you think of that person? Make a list.

_____ is _____
     (Name)

_____

_____

_____

6. What is it that you don't want to experience with that person again?

I don't ever want to _____

_____

_____

_____

The Turnaround for Number 6

The turnaround for statement number 6 is a little different from the other turnarounds. "I don't ever want to experience an argument with Paul again" turns around to "*I am willing* to experience an argument with Paul again and *I look forward* to experiencing an argument with Paul again."

The turnaround for number 6 is about welcoming all your thoughts and experiences with open arms. If you feel any resistance to a thought, your Work is not done. When you can honestly look forward to experiences that have been uncomfortable, there is no longer anything to fear in life—you see everything as a gift that can bring love, laughter, and peace to your life.

Practicing Staying in Your Own Business

Exercise

When you feel angry or upset, and hear yourself saying or think-ing: "He [she] should _____, he shouldn't _____, he needs to _____," and so on, stop and ask: *Is that true? Can I know that about him? Am I out of my business?* Then turn it around to: *I should _____, I shouldn't _____, I need to _____,* and so on. Give yourself the prescription you were going to give someone else and see what happens.

Exercise

When you have the urge to give unrequested advice (whether aloud or in your mind) or you find yourself thinking that you know what's right for someone, ask yourself, *Whose business am I in? Did anyone ask for my opinion? Can I know what's right for someone else?* Then listen to your own advice, and know that you're the one it's meant for. Stay in your own business and be happy.

ACKNOWLEDGMENTS

Hundreds of people—too many to name—contributed to this book by bringing inquiry into their lives and sending in their results by e-mail. A few of their accounts appear here anonymously. As for the manuscript itself, Carol Williams and John Tarrant each gave devotion and acute editorial skills to the task of putting words to an essentially wordless experience. Belinda Fernandez read early drafts of the book, tried out the exercises, and reported back with accurate and encouraging comments. Near the end of the process, Stephen (The Whiz) Mitchell seated himself midstream in a rapids of words and brought instant smooth flow. At Harmony Books, Shaye Areheart was always encouraging, and Kim Meisner made keen editorial suggestions. Heartfelt thanks to all.

CONTACT INFORMATION

Byron Katie presents The Work in person at free public events, weekend intensives, and nine-day schools in the United States and Europe. For current information, go to www.thework.com and look for the Upcoming Events page.

    If you don't have access to the Internet, contact:

Byron Katie International

P.O. Box 2110

Manhattan Beach, CA 90267

Phone: 310-760-9000

Fax: 310-760-9008

www.thework.com

E-mail: info@thework.com

Read More About Inquiry

Loving What Is: Four Questions That Can Change Your Life
By Byron Katie with Stephen Mitchell

Byron Katie's first book offers detailed instruction on doing The Work and many powerful examples of people doing The Work with Katie on a wide range of problems, from money troubles to terrorist attacks. *Loving What Is* is widely available in paperback and as an audiobook.